Somatic Healing for Women

Everyday Practices to Release Trauma, Restore Emotional Balance, and Reclaim Your Life

R.V. Brown

Copyright © 2025 by R.V. Brown

All rights reserved. No part of this book may be copied, reproduced, stored, or transmitted in any form or by any means—electronic, mechanical, photocopying, recording, or otherwise—without the prior written permission of the author or publisher, except for brief quotations used in reviews, articles, or educational materials.

ISBN (Hardcover): 979-8-9993160-0-4 | ISBN (Paperback): 979-8-9993160-1-1
ISBN (eBook): 979-8-9993160-2-8

Published by **Rocket Publishing LLC**

Printed in the United States of America
First Edition, 2025
Cover and interior design by Rocket Studios LLC
Layout and formatting by Vellum

Legal Notice:

This book is copyright protected and intended for personal use only. You may not edit, distribute, sell, quote, or paraphrase any portion of the content without written permission from the author or publisher.

Disclaimer:

The information in this book is provided for educational and informational purposes only and does not constitute professional advice. The author is not a licensed therapist, physician, or medical practitioner. This book is not intended to diagnose, treat, or cure any condition. Readers are advised to consult with a qualified healthcare professional before applying any techniques or suggestions presented.

By reading this book, you agree that the author and publisher are not liable for any damages or losses incurred from its use, whether direct or indirect, including but not limited to errors, omissions, or inaccuracies.

To my husband;

*Thank you for being my northern star.
Your love has been a guiding light
along every path we've walked together.*

*I love you yesterday, today, tomorrow…
Always.*

CONTENTS

Introduction	vii
1. UNDERSTANDING SOMATIC THERAPY	1
The Body and Trauma: Interconnected Pathways	2
Somatic Therapy: A New Approach to Healing	4
But…I Already Go to Therapy	6
The Decision to Medicate	7
2. BUILDING SOMATIC AWARENESS	13
Recognizing Body Signals of Stress and Trauma	18
Connecting Physical Sensations to Emotions	21
3. GROUNDING TECHNIQUES FOR EVERYDAY USE	25
Sensory Awareness: Engaging the Five Senses	29
Immediate Grounding Practices for High-Stress Moments	32
4. MINDFULNESS AND EMBODIMENT	37
Mindfulness Meditation for Emotional Regulation	40
Short and Effective Mindfulness Routines	45
5. CREATIVE EXPRESSION IN SOMATIC THERAPY	49
Journaling for Emotional Release and Discovery	53
Sample Letter Prompts	55
Music and Movement: Creative Pathways to Healing	57
6. PERSONALIZING SOMATIC EXERCISES	61
Low-Energy Days: Gentle Somatic Approaches	64
Creating a Personalized Somatic Routine	66
7. BUILDING EMOTIONAL RESILIENCE	69
Techniques for Building Resilience	74
Self-Regulation: Managing Emotional Reactions	79

8. INTEGRATING SOMATIC THERAPY INTO
   DAILY LIFE ... 83
   Consistency is key! ... 85
   Mindful Breaks: Incorporating Somatic Moments
   at Work ... 87
   Evening Practices for Rest and Reflection ... 89

9. CREATIVITY AS A THERAPEUTIC TOOL ... 93
   I'm not artistic. What can I do? ... 94
   Exploring Movement and Dance Therapy ... 97
   Writing as a Therapeutic Journey ... 98
   Writing Exercise Ideas ... 100

10. ADDRESSING SKEPTICISM AND BARRIERS ... 103
    Let's Get A Little Science-y ... 105
    Fear of Re-traumatization in Therapy ... 107
    Making Time for Somatic Practices in Busy Lives ... 109
    Build Your Practice Schedule ... 110

11. CASE STUDIES AND SUCCESS STORIES ... 111
    Diverse Journeys: Somatic Therapy Across Cultures ... 119

12. ENHANCING THE MIND-BODY CONNECTION ... 123
    Physical Manifestations of Emotional States ... 125
    Harnessing the Mind-Body Link for Healing ... 127

13. NAVIGATING CHRONIC CONDITIONS ... 131
    Using Your Breath ... 133
    Create A Pain Management Plan ... 134
    Coping with Chronic Illness: Mindful Living ... 135
    Enhancing Quality of Life with Somatic Practices ... 137

14. BUILDING COMMUNITY AND SUPPORT ... 141
    Online Communities: Sharing and Learning
    Together ... 144
    The Power of Group Sessions ... 147
    Where to Begin ... 148

15. REFLECTION AND INTEGRATION ... 151
    Integrating Insights into Everyday Life ... 155

16. ADVANCED SOMATIC TECHNIQUES ... 159
    Somatic Experiencing: Deep Dive into Healing ... 161
    Integrating Somatic Practices with Other Therapies ... 163

17. MAINTAINING MOMENTUM 167
   Sustaining Your Somatic Practice for Long-term
   Wellness 168

   Afterword 173
   Make a Difference with Your Review 177
   References 179

INTRODUCTION

"Do one thing every day that scares you."

— ELEANOR ROOSEVELT

Just before the pandemic, I heard a guest speaker at a women's conference. She was around my age and spoke of her childhood trauma. After decades of carrying the weight of her past, she felt hollow and disconnected, like a stranger in her own skin. Her therapist suggested somatic yoga to help with her physical pain. And, after committing to practice 5 days a week, she began to trust her body again. The story of her transformation revealed options that I never knew existed. It left such an impact on me that I wanted to share this healing path with other women.

You may be thinking, "That's all well and good. But, what is somatic therapy, and what does it have to do with me?" Simply put, somatic therapy focuses on the mind-body connection and

INTRODUCTION

teaches us that trauma is stored in both our minds and our bodies. It uses physical sensations and movements to release emotions and tension that have been stored in our bodies since our trauma occurred. This is so effective because it addresses you as a whole, acknowledging that your physical and emotional experiences are deeply connected.

Ironically, after decades of letting my emotions run rampant in my life, I started therapy in my late 40s. I had been in a state of constant stress and anxiety for about 8 or 9 years, and my health was steadily declining. We were in the process of making a major move when I decided it was time to seek professional talk therapy. I made a promise to myself that I would seek therapy once we were relocated. At that time, I had completely forgotten about the speaker from the women's conference. I was in the throes of perimenopause. I felt sad all the time. We were making a move we had planned for years, and the pieces of our plan were coming together while I was falling apart. I was on the struggle bus, and there was no bus stop in sight.

Four days after moving into our new house, in a new state, with a new job in a completely different role, I walked into my first individual talk therapy session. It was one of the first times, in a long time, that I remember keeping a promise to myself, and when I left, I wondered why I had waited so long.

As my therapist and I worked through the ways my body has been affected by trauma, I learned about the direct link between our physical and emotional selves. Each of us has arrived at this place in our lives due to various emotional and physical experiences. But even two people with the same trauma may process it very differently. This is the very reason that somatic healing is so successful among women. Women of different ages and from

INTRODUCTION

various backgrounds. Women with high school diplomas and women with prestigious degrees. Women. All of us. Each of us.

This book is the book that I needed in my 30s when I first decided it was time to ditch the baggage I was still carrying with me from childhood, trauma, and loss. This book is the book I needed in my 40s when I finally went to therapy for myself, and wondered every day why I didn't start sooner. This book is the book that I still need today, and every day, as I strive to be a little better than I was yesterday and the day before. And, more importantly, this book is the book I hope will give all women, at every stage, the permission to say, "I am not okay...But I will be."

If you've experienced PTSD (Post-Traumatic Stress Disorder), trauma, burnout, chronic fatigue, anxiety, or depression, please keep reading. If you crave emotional regulation, suffer from chronic illness, are navigating menopause, or feel disconnected from your sense of self, you are not here by chance. I see you. I empathize with you. And, I understand that you may have unique challenges. We each have a different story and a unique path forward. You belong.

Somatic therapy will teach you to build a customizable practice made specifically for you. One that respects your individual experiences, acknowledges your strengths, provides grace in times of weakness, and charts a path to healing that is compassionate, empowering, and adjustable to ebb and flow with your ever-changing needs.

The book is organized into sections that guide you through different aspects of somatic therapy. We will explore practical applications and engage with interactive elements that will introduce you to the various ways you can build your personal plan. Whether you're new to somatic therapy or have some experience, there's something here for you.

INTRODUCTION

Inside, you'll find creative practices that integrate mindfulness, breathwork, movement, art, journaling, and various other means of creative expression. These elements are designed to support you while making the process engaging and meaningful.

There is no special equipment to buy. No strict schedules that require you to rise at dawn, unless you want to. There is no one way to do it right, and no single path to healing. All I ask is that you remain open to new experiences, do your best each day, and prioritize healing your heart. You are the author of your next chapter, and my goal is to equip you with the tools to make it your **best** chapter yet.

Throughout the book, you'll find interactive ways to practice what you've read. The exercises are not mandatory, but they will help you determine what works best for you in real time.

As you read through the book, do your best to engage with the material. Dig deep. The practices shared in this book can help you reclaim your body and transform your life. So, come as you are. This book will meet you there, with me…together. You are welcome, and you are valued.

Now, let's begin.

CHAPTER 1
UNDERSTANDING SOMATIC THERAPY

"Every new beginning comes from some other beginning's end."

— LUCIUS ANNAEUS SENECA

When we think about trauma, we generally focus on the emotional scars it leaves behind. But have you ever considered how your body holds onto these experiences?

J.L. Moreno did. And, it might surprise you to learn what he discovered. Ready? Our bodies remember what our minds try to forget. Let me say that again because it is *so* important…our bodies *remember* what our minds try to *forget*. When you put it that way, it's no wonder healing is such a process. But this is the premise of somatic therapy. Somatic therapy views the body as an active participant in our emotional lives.

THE BODY AND TRAUMA: INTERCONNECTED PATHWAYS

The human body's response to trauma is complex and deeply rooted in our biology. Biology! Ew! Don't worry, I won't get too deep. When you experience a traumatic event, your body instinctively activates the fight-or-flight response. Most people know this reaction and may have considered how they might react in certain situations.

Your system automatically becomes flooded with adrenaline and cortisol, preparing you to either confront the threat or escape it. This response is designed to protect you from harm. Pretty ingenious, if you think about it. But what happens when the threat is gone?

For many, these stress hormones linger, creating a state of chronic hyperarousal that shows up in your body as tension, anxiety, or even panic attacks. Your muscles may remain tight, and your heart rate may be elevated, as if your body is constantly on high alert. This ongoing state of stress can be exhausting and damaging, reinforcing the emotional pain you might already feel.

But trauma doesn't just reside in your conscious memory; it also lives in what we call somatic memory. This means that your body retains memories of trauma, even if your mind does not recall them consciously. It's why certain sounds, smells, or environments can trigger intense emotional reactions when we least expect them. These are emotional flashbacks, and your body will react as if the trauma is happening all over again.

You might feel a knot in your stomach, a lump in your throat, or a sudden tension in your shoulders. If you are in the presence of others, you may feel the need to escape or leave a social function. These sensations are your body's way of communicating any unresolved emotions and stressors. It's trying to *protect you* from the thing that caused the *original emotional trauma*. Addressing these somatic memories is critical for healing, processing, and releasing the trauma held within you.

> "...your body doesn't just react; it remembers."

The star of this show is your nervous system, which plays the leading role in how your body responds to trauma. The sympathetic and parasympathetic nervous systems work hand-in-hand to keep your stress levels under control. Sounds technical? Stick with me, and I'll explain a little further.

The sympathetic nervous system tells your body to be super alert, while the parasympathetic nervous system helps calm and reset it. In trauma, this balance can get…well…unbalanced, which leads to dysregulation. This is why your emotions can sometimes feel all over the place.

Techniques such as vagus nerve stimulation can help restore this balance. The vagus nerve is on the parasympathetic team. It starts at the brain stem and goes down to the abdomen, and it's responsible for a lot of important things that happen automatically in our bodies. Things like breathing, digestion, heart rate, mood, and more.

It's like a bridge between your mind and your body, and if you stimulate it, you can activate the parasympathetic (calming) response, reducing stress and promoting healing. Now, can you see where we're going with this one?

Parasympathetic\nBody at rest		Sympathetic\nEmergencies
Constricts pupils	**EYES**	Dialates pupils
Beat more slowly	**HEART**	Beats faster and stronger
Constricts airways	**LUNGS**	Relaxes airways which lets you breathe more deeply
Stimulates digestion	**STOMACH**	Inhibits digestion
Reduces blood flow to skeletal muscles	**MUSCLES**	Increases blood flow to skeletal muscles

The mind-body connection is the cornerstone of somatic therapy. Stress-induced headaches, gastrointestinal flare-ups, heart palpitations, and other physical symptoms are reminders of how closely connected your emotional state is to your physical health. When you experience stress or trauma, your body doesn't just react; it remembers. And, let's face it…your body's got a really good memory.

SOMATIC THERAPY: A NEW APPROACH TO HEALING

Where traditional therapy focuses primarily on verbal communication, somatic therapy helps you engage with the physical sensations, movements, and awareness that are happening inside your body. It's like learning a new language that is spoken with movement, gestures, and feelings.

Body awareness exercises are the perfect beginning to your somatic practice. These exercises help you notice sensations and tensions you may be feeling without passing judgment. Let me give you an example.

Body Awareness Exercise

- Imagine standing barefoot on the kitchen tile.
- Your eyes are closed.
- You can feel the cool tile under your feet.
- Now, take a deep breath.

This type of awareness is a great starting point, teaching you to be present with your body in new ways.

While many therapies focus on a cognitive (knowledge-based) approach, such as thinking and reasoning, somatic therapy focuses on physical and emotional healing. And, since we know now that trauma affects both the mind and the body, we can wager that healing should address both as well.

When we recognize that words alone may not capture the depth of one's experiences, we invite non-verbal communication to have a part in the process. For instance, when you're overwhelmed with emotion, your body might express what words cannot. Maybe you've experienced trembling hands, unwelcome tears, or a deep, audible sigh. Have you ever cried because you were frustrated…not sad, but didn't understand why? Have you ever felt an overwhelming urge to scream or hit something when you aren't a violent person? Somatic therapy teaches you to listen and respond to these cues.

One of the biggest advantages is the reduction in chronic pain. Many individuals who have experienced trauma report persistent physical discomfort, often unexplained by medical tests. By learning to release the tension and stress stored in their muscles, they experience considerable pain relief. This reduction in pain can help with mobility and give individuals a renewed sense of freedom.

Emotional regulation also improves as you learn to identify and process your emotions in a safe and supportive way. You become more attuned to your feelings, granting you the ability to **respond,** rather than **react,** to emotional triggers. As an added bonus, you'll build body awareness that guides you through your physical and emotional experiences with greater confidence.

BUT...I ALREADY GO TO THERAPY

Great! You've already chosen to prioritize your health and healing. Let's take it one step further. Traditional talk therapy is often the chosen entryway on the path of healing. But for some whose trauma is deeply rooted in their bodies, talk therapy alone can seem somewhat inadequate, and occasionally triggering. Talk therapy is a great way to explore your feelings and thoughts, but it may not completely tackle the physical symptoms that trauma can cause.

> *Translation:* While you might feel emotional relief, your body could still be holding onto those experiences, leaving some of your physical discomfort unaddressed.

Think about it. You're sitting across from your therapist while your mind recounts your trauma. As good as it may feel to **talk** through it verbally, *your body craves the same physical release.* Without a somatic practice, the body will continue carrying the weight of that stress and tension. This absence of physical engagement can hold you back from complete healing and growth.

THE DECISION TO MEDICATE

Before stepping into this part of the conversation, let's pause. The decision to medicate should not be influenced or dissuaded solely by the words of any self-help book. The choice to use prescription, herbal, or holistic methods to aid in your healing process is one that should be made personally with the help of your healthcare provider.

While prescription medication can be necessary for managing overwhelming symptoms and beneficial for a wide variety of mental health diagnoses, it is **not** something I will weigh in on.

The purpose of this section is to speak to the advantages of **including somatic practices** in healing, **whether medication is part of your plan or not**. If you choose to move forward holistically, without the assistance of any pharmaceuticals, please proceed to Chapter 2. If medication has a place in your path, or if you are unsure, please continue on.

If you are currently taking medication for the management of your symptoms or diagnosis, or if your healthcare provider has recommended medication as a next step, please take some time to research how somatic practices can aid in that healing.

As a member of the medication population, I can attest to the positive impact of combining talk therapy and somatic practices when prescription medications are recommended. This full-bodied approach helped me better manage symptoms between talk therapy visits, while building my somatic practice. It takes time and patience to cultivate a practice that fits your specific needs. So, do what is best for you at this particular time and place in your life. You can always pivot and reassess, if necessary.

"...remember that healing is not a one-size-fits-all process."

While medication is part of my personal journey, I had a particularly difficult time coming off my antidepressant. The withdrawal symptoms were not something I expected to have such a complete grip on my life. I had unexplained stomach nausea, cramping, sadness, headache, debilitating brain zaps, and anxiety...more anxiety than I've ever been able to identify as such.

One particular Friday, I had a big project at work. My husband was working from home that day. We had contractors coming to do some work outside, and the dogs were losing their minds over the strangers in our backyard. My brain zaps were horrible with the added stress of the morning, so my concentration was in the toilet. I was also fighting an asthma flare-up and had taken my inhaler a few moments before.

Emotionally, I was spent, and it was only 10:30 in the morning. Every time I tried to focus on work, I kept getting interrupted. My husband called out from downstairs asking me to block the stairs off from the dogs, and I lost it.

I grabbed the gate and slammed it onto the stairs with all the gusto of a three-year-old having a colossal meltdown. Then, as if in slow motion, I watched as the gate sailed down the wooden staircase and onto the wooden floor below, making my husband jump to avoid it. I immediately knew I had overreacted...BIG TIME...and I instantly regretted it.

He simply looked up at me and back down at the floor. Then he shook his head in disbelief before walking away. His "disappointment" immediately flooded me with shame. I couldn't believe I lost it over that one simple request.

Over the next hour or so, that shame ruminated until I'd relived every bit of shame I felt over the last 40+ years...NO JOKE! The shame train took me straight back to first grade. First grade. It was a subject that my therapist and I had been discussing over the last several sessions.

Like any good introvert with anxiety, I withdrew into myself, and the ruminating continued. The brain zaps continued to worsen due to the added stress, and my head continued to pound incessantly.

I lay down for my lunch hour, secretly hoping my husband would come downstairs and hug me and say it was okay. I couldn't look at him for fear of seeing that disappointment again. That simple look triggered shame that left me with the catastrophizing fear of abandonment after 30 years of marriage. I was spiraling. Mayday! Mayday! Crash and burn.

This, my friends, is how trauma teams up with anxiety to morph one tiny event from today into a full-blown "catastrophe" fueled by events from your past. And, not just your immediate past... way, way back...Like, childhood back.

This was not a "him" problem. This was a "me" problem. All I wanted was for him to tell me that he forgave me. That he wasn't disappointed in me. That he understood what I was feeling, and that he wasn't going anywhere. That's ultimately what I needed…I needed to know he wouldn't leave me over a baby gate and a 50-year-old temper tantrum.

Ladies…hear me when I say those scars run deep. And, you know what I've realized over 31 years of marriage? No matter how hard I've tried to avoid it, I've been punishing my husband for the sins of other men since we started dating 34 years ago! How sad.

I am eternally thankful he loved me enough to stay during those initial years when I didn't know how to have a real relationship. But it is not fair of me to want something from him that he doesn't know I need. Read that again. *It's not fair of me to want something from him that he doesn't know I need.*

You see, I was hoping he would come to comfort me and ease my fears. But he had no idea what was happening inside me, so he had no idea *how* to help, and he certainly had no idea that I *wanted and needed* him to help. I was holding him to a standard that he didn't know existed. And, it wasn't fair to him or to me.

We eventually had time alone that evening, and I was able to apologize and do my best to explain. Not to make excuses, but to help him understand what was happening to me internally. It was humbling, and horrifying, and necessary. So, so necessary. Want to know what I did next? I messaged my therapist the very next morning to schedule an appointment.

The thing is, our partners (or other loved ones) don't know all the battle scars we carry. Even if they walked *right beside us* on the battlefield, their bodies process things differently than we do, and our emotional scars are often far worse than any physical scars we could imagine.

I've often wished we could "stitch up" an emotional scar like we are stitched after a physical injury. If it were that simple, I could look at that mark near my heart and say, "Oh yeah…that's my childhood abandonment issues, but it's all healed up now. Look at me all put-back-together and strong." We both know that's not going to happen.

But, do you know what didn't cross my mind about that theory? Physical scars. Ask anyone who's had a major surgery (where are my c-section ladies) and they will tell you that physical scars leave painful scar tissue behind. There is just no escaping it.

We all have scars, and we must learn how to care for those sensitive areas of our lives, whether physical or emotional, so we can heal completely.

CHAPTER 2
BUILDING SOMATIC AWARENESS

"The paradox of trauma is that it has both the power to destroy and the power to transform and resurrect."

— PETER A. LEVINE

What would you give to wake up each morning feeling truly connected to your body? This might sound like a distant dream, especially if you've spent years feeling detached or at odds with your physical self. However, this connection is achievable through somatic awareness, a practice that stresses the importance of listening *deeply* to your body.

Your body communicates constantly, and learning to understand this language can make all the difference in your healing process. Somatic awareness starts with the simple act of being present and noticing what's happening in your body, without judgment.

It's about tuning into those whispers of discomfort or unease, acknowledging them, and exploring what they might be telling you about your emotional world.

One way to build your awareness is through body scan meditation. This is a great exercise for beginners, teaching you to be present with your body so you can begin to understand where you are storing tension and stress.

Body Scan Meditation

Find a comfortable seat. You can sit cross-legged on the floor, in a chair with your feet flat on the ground, or you can lie down. Get comfortable. Take a deep breath. As you exhale, close your eyes. Beginning with your head, mentally scan your body. You will move from the top of your head to your ears, face, shoulders, arms, torso, stomach, hips, legs, feet, and toes. As you move through your body, observe any sensations you might be feeling. Don't try to change them. We are just observing. No more, no less. You might feel warmth in your chest, a tingling in your feet, or tension in your shoulders. Each sensation is a clue, a piece of the puzzle that makes up your current state of being. Focus on your breath and breathe deeply a few times before slowly opening your eyes.

By practicing body scan meditation regularly, you develop a deeper understanding of how your body responds to different emotions and situations. This practice can be especially useful for processing trauma, as it encourages a gentle exploration of the body's stored experiences.

Mindfulness expert Jon Kabat-Zinn describes this practice as "falling awake," suggesting that it heightens your awareness of the present moment and helps you become more attuned to your body's needs. Don't be discouraged if you don't "feel" everything at once. Identifying your body's signals happens over time spent with yourself.

In addition to body scan meditation, paying attention to your breathing patterns can boost somatic awareness. Breathing is an automatic process, yet it often changes subtly in response to stress or relaxation. By tuning into your natural breathing rhythm, you learn about your emotional state. Is your breath shallow and rapid? This might indicate anxiety or tension. Is it deep and slow? This suggests calmness and relaxation. Simply noticing these patterns can help you identify when you're feeling stressed or when you're at ease, alerting you to take the appropriate actions, even if that means no action at all.

Techniques like progressive muscle relaxation and guided imagery can also strengthen your connection with your body. Progressive muscle relaxation involves intentionally tensing and then relaxing different muscle groups, which can help you become more aware of where you hold tension. As you practice, you'll likely notice patterns, such as clenched jaws or tight fists, that might correspond to emotional stressors.

Guided imagery, on the other hand, uses the power of visualization to create soothing mental images that promote relaxation and healing. By imagining a peaceful scene or a place where you feel safe, you can shift your body's stress response and cultivate a sense of calm.

Guided imagery was one of the first somatic practices that my therapist used during trauma therapy. In that session, we were working on identifying my safe space. As she walked me through some of the aspects of "creating" that safe space within, my heart immediately settled on Muir Woods National Monument in Marin County, California. I've loved the redwoods and sequoias for most of my adult life, and Muir Woods was a place I could easily step into in my mind.

The smell of the forest air, the crisp sound of the leaves crunching beneath my feet, the way my feet moved along the uneven path on the trails, the birds singing, the hushed voices of patrons enjoying the beauty of these gentle giants…I could go on and on. It's fully immersive for me, and it brings me such immeasurable peace. It was one of the most transformative moments in my life, and it lives rent-free in my brain.

Can you think of a place that can transport you in this way? Finding your own personal Muir Woods is a pivotal step in your somatic process. Let's take a moment to explore that a little more.

Guided Imagery Exercise

What is your place of peace? Is there a place or memory that affects you so deeply that you can visualize everything as if you were there? What does it look like? What sounds are associated with it? What do you feel internally when you are there? Does it have a smell? Is there a food or drink that brings you back to this place? How can you use this information to create a safe space where you can retreat during your healing process? Focus on that place the next time your emotions feel like too much to bear.

Listening to your body through somatic awareness and tuning into your body's signals can improve emotional regulation and manage stress more effectively. This practice helps with self-love and self-compassion, as you learn to accept and care for your body as it is...without judgment. It also enables you to detect stress signals early and address them before they escalate. This proactive approach to self-care can improve your resilience, helping you handle life's challenges with greater ease.

To support this process, consider keeping a journal to document your somatic experiences. Use descriptive journaling prompts to capture the sensations and emotions you notice during your somatic practices. Reviewing your entries over time can reveal patterns of how your body responds to different situations.

Journaling Prompts

- "What sensations did I notice during my body scan today? How did they change as I focused on them?"
- "Describe a moment when my breath felt particularly tense or relaxed. What was happening in my life at that time?"
- "What patterns have I observed in my body when I'm feeling stressed or calm? How can I use this knowledge to support myself?"

Using these prompts on a regular basis can help you understand your body's language, as you build a better relationship with yourself.

RECOGNIZING BODY SIGNALS OF STRESS AND TRAUMA

Stress and trauma often make themselves known through physical symptoms before we consciously recognize them. Think about the last time you felt overwhelmed. Were your neck and shoulders tense? Did you have a back ache? How was your breathing?

These symptoms are common ways that stress shows up in the body...kind of like an internal alarm system. When you're stressed, muscle tension and tightness are frequent visitors, often taking up residence in your neck, shoulders, and back. This change is your body's way of signaling you that something is not okay. You might find yourself breathing faster, or your breath becomes shallow. These changes in your breathing pattern can exacerbate any feelings of anxiety or panic that you might be experiencing.

Another common complaint is digestive distress. Stomach churning, nausea, and sudden loss of appetite are all physical symptoms of your body's response to stress and trauma. Recognizing when and how your body responds is the first step in addressing the root causes.

As mentioned in Chapter 1, when we encounter stressful situations, our bodies go into fight-or-flight mode. This causes your body to release adrenaline and cortisol. These are survival hormones that prepare you to face a threat, real or perceived, by increasing your heart rate and blood pressure. While this response is helpful in short bursts, chronic stress keeps your body in a heightened state of alertness, which can be very damaging over time. It's like your body is constantly revving its engine, even when you're sitting still. This unnecessary wear and tear on your cardiovascular system makes stress management a mental and physical health priority.

"Your body has a lot to tell you…"

Being able to differentiate between general stress indicators and those specific to trauma is important. Stress is a part of everyday life, but trauma leaves deeper imprints on the body.

When you experience a trauma trigger, your body might exhibit hyperarousal symptoms. You might break out into a sweat, notice a racing heart, or have a feeling of being "on edge." These responses are more intense than typical stress reactions and can feel overwhelming.

Identifying your unique triggers is an important exercise. It could be a particular sound, a place, or a specific smell that brings you back to a traumatic moment. Recognizing these triggers gives you a chance to pause, prepare, and respond in a way that reduces their impact.

Identifying Triggers

Learning what triggers you is a very personal process. While some triggers might be common with PTSD, others are very specific to a traumatic event. Do any of the following examples ignite a trauma response in your body?

- Feeling unsafe
- Abandonment
- Arguements
- Firearms
- Unexpected or loud noises
- Rejection
- Unfair blame
- Busy schedule
- Feeling helpless
- Being ignored
- Being judged
- Condescending tone
- Crowds of people
- Tight spaces
- Specific sounds: horn, screaming, crying, loud crash, etc.
- Certain places: parking garage, mall, airport, doctor's office, etc.
- Specific scents: blood, hospitals, cologne, cigar smoke, alcohol, etc.

Other triggers I have noticed:

_____

_____

_____

When you notice these signals, taking proactive steps can help you regain control. Below are a couple of options for combating these feelings and reclaiming your body.

1. **DEEP BREATHING EXERCISES** help slow your heart rate and calm the nervous system, bringing your body back to a more relaxed state. If you find yourself in a stressful situation, focus on taking deep, measured breaths or envisioning your safe space. This helps to counteract the fight-or-flight response.
2. **GROUNDING TECHNIQUES** help to anchor you in the present moment. This might involve focusing on the sensation of your feet on the ground or the texture of an object in your hand. This redirects your attention away from unsettling thoughts and back to the safety of the here and now.

Understanding your body and its signals allows you to respond to stress and trauma with resilience. Your body has a lot to tell you. Isn't it time you started to listen?

CONNECTING PHYSICAL SENSATIONS TO EMOTIONS

Have you ever felt a tightness in your chest when you're anxious or a queasy stomach when fear strikes? These aren't just random physical reactions; they are your body's way of communicating how you're feeling emotionally. This delicate dance between your physical sensations and emotions is key to understanding yourself on a deeper level. Recognizing these connections entices you to explore what's happening beneath the surface. When you start to observe and decode these signals, you stop reacting to your emotions and start engaging with them.

To map these connections, try creating a personal body-emotion map. This can be a powerful exercise. Begin by noting the physical sensations you frequently experience and the emotions that accompany them.

Remember, this process is about observing. We are putting the pieces of your puzzle together. No analyzing or judging allowed. You might find that certain emotions manifest in specific parts of your body. Perhaps stress always feels like a weight on your shoulders, or sadness feels like a sinking sensation in your chest. By charting these patterns, you'll begin to understand how your body responds to your emotions.

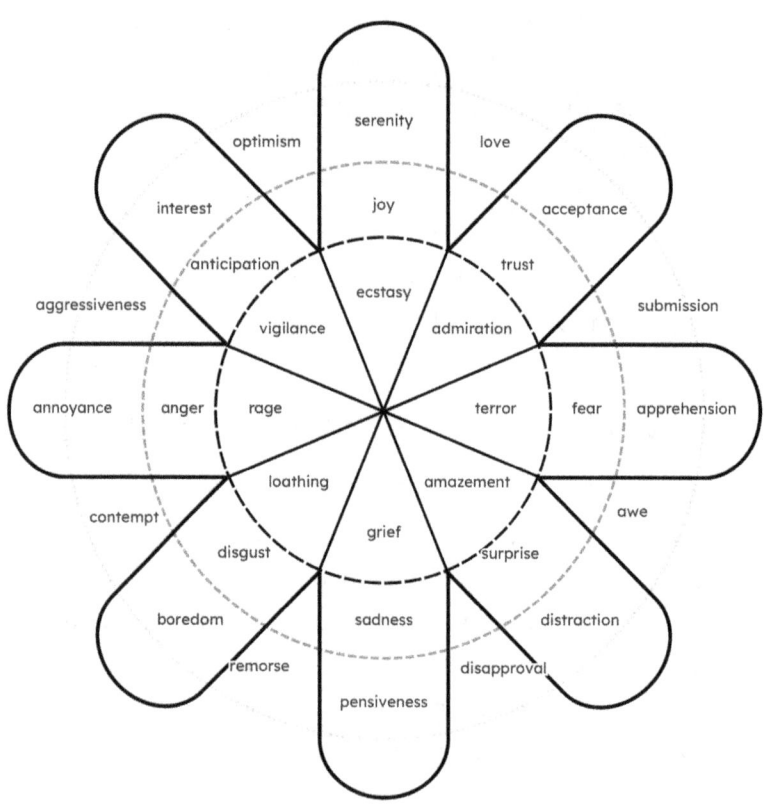

Reflective exercises can take things a step further. A quick pause throughout your day to check in with your body, noting any sensations and emotions that arise, can reveal patterns that help you anticipate and manage emotional responses.

Emotional awareness acknowledges and validates your emotions, holding space for them to be felt and understood. Emotional validation techniques teach you to state your feelings without judgment. When you say to yourself, "It's okay to feel this way," you recognize that your emotions are valid, even if they are uncomfortable.

Sometimes, these emotions linger in the body, stored as tension or discomfort. Releasing them through movement can be incredibly liberating. Dance or movement therapy encourages you to express emotions physically, moving through them rather than feeling stuck.

Whether you're swaying to music or gently stretching, these activities permit you to embody your feelings and release them in a way that words sometimes cannot express.

Another powerful way to process emotions is through vocal expression exercises. Your voice is a tool for release. Using it for speaking or singing can help move our internal emotions out into the world.

Try letting yourself vocalize what you're feeling, even if it's just a simple sound. This practice isn't about performance; it's about expression. By giving voice to your emotions, you acknowledge and permit them to flow, reducing their hold over you. This kind of expression honors all of your feelings…even the ones we have been taught to hold in.

5 Minute Dance Party

Go to a neutral place and set a timer for 5 minutes. Crank up your favorite music, and have a dance party for one. Okay, okay, you can invite the kids if you must.

Dancing not your thing? Try belting out your favorite song. Don't just sing the lyrics. Feel the lyrics. Experience the words and the emotion behind them, like you're the artist performing on a sold-out stage.

As you explore the connections between your physical sensations and emotions, remember that this process is personal and unique. There is no right or wrong way to experience your feelings.

As cliche as it sounds, let your body be your guide. Give yourself the time and space to learn how to heal and thrive. Embrace this part of the process, knowing that each step you take towards fully understanding yourself is a step towards living your best life.

CHAPTER 3
GROUNDING TECHNIQUES FOR EVERYDAY USE

"Be like a tree. Stay grounded. Connect with your roots. Turn over a new leaf. Bend before you break. Enjoy your unique natural beauty. Keep growing."

— JANNE RAPTIS

Ever wonder why the beach has such a peaceful effect on people? When you're standing on the shore, feeling the gentle waves flowing over your feet, it's easy to fall into a more relaxed state of mind. You can feel the ocean's steady, calming breeze mirroring a powerful tool we all possess...our breath.

Breathwork is one of the most accessible grounding tools available. It is a direct path to calm your mind and steady your body. When life feels overwhelming and the chaos of emotions rises, your breath can be an anchor, bringing you back to a place of peace. Many of us, however, forget to breathe deeply, especially when stressed. Instead, we take short and shallow breaths, which can heighten anxiety and tension. Learning to control your breath can provide immediate relief in challenging situations.

One of the most effective techniques is diaphragmatic breathing, often called **"belly breathing."** This method encourages you to breathe deeply from your belly rather than your chest. This simple exercise helps utilize the diaphragm fully, promoting relaxation and reducing stress. Let's try it together now.

BELLY BREATHING

Another option is the *4-7-8 breathing method*. This rhythmic breathing exercise involves timing your breath. First, you inhale for four seconds. Then, you hold the breath for seven seconds. Lastly, you exhale for eight seconds. This technique redirects your focus as you concentrate on counting out your breathwork. It can be particularly helpful in calming the mind, especially at bedtime.

4-7-8 BREATHING

Structured breathing exercises, like *box breathing*, are great calming exercises that can be practiced discreetly from just about anywhere. Box breathing is all about the number four: Inhale for a count of four. Hold for four. Exhale for four. Pause for four. Then repeat. This method is excellent for finding focus.

BOX BREATHING

Alternate nostril breathing is a yoga technique also known as Nadi Shodhana. It is a breath control practice called pranayama. This technique involves closing one nostril while inhaling through the other and switching sides for the exhale. It may seem like an odd approach to grounding, but this technique balances your body's energy and strengthens cardiovascular function. Who knew breathing exercises could be so interesting?

ALTERNATE NOSTRIL BREATHING

When you engage in controlled breathing practices, you activate the parasympathetic nervous system, which is responsible for "rest and digest" activities. This slows your heart rate and lowers your blood pressure, counteracting the adrenaline rush that comes with stress. It's like hitting the reset button on your body's stress response.

Controlled breathing is also great for reducing cortisol levels. Left unchecked, the stress hormone Cortisol can wreak havoc on your health. Regular practice of these techniques promotes relaxation and strengthens your body's ability to stop the damaging effects of stress..

Incorporating breathwork into your daily routine can transform these exercises from occasional practices into lifelong habits that support your continued health. Consider starting your day with a morning breathing ritual. Before getting out of bed, take a few moments to practice diaphragmatic (belly) breathing, setting a calm and focused tone for the day ahead.

Set a reminder on your phone for short breathing breaks during your day. These can be as simple as taking a minute to practice box breathing at your desk, or while sitting in line at carpool. This quick mental reset increases productivity and reduces fatigue. And, let's face it, fatigue is something most adult women are well acquainted with. If you know, you know.

Did you know?

Fatigue is among the most frequently reported medical complaints in women over 30.

According to the University of Miami Health System, about 63% of women in the U.S. report feeling tired or fatigued during the day. I'd be willing to bet the other 37% were passed out from exhaustion and couldn't respond to the survey.

Seriously, though, 63% is terrifying! When I think of the women in my circle, no one walks around talking about how much energy and stamina they have. Quite often, complaints of chronic fatigue will be the entry point to diagnosing other issues like hormone imbalances, chronic stress, trauma, or autoimmune conditions. And, you guessed it, fatigue is deeply connected to your emotional and somatic health.

Breathing Break Schedule

- Morning Ritual: Begin with five minutes of diaphragmatic (belly) breathing before starting your day.
- Mid-Morning: Take a two-minute box breathing break during your morning coffee.
- Lunch Break: Before eating, practice the 4-7-8 breathing technique to relax and digest better.
- Afternoon: Use alternate nostril breathing for three minutes to restore your focus.
- Evening Wind-Down: Conclude your day with five minutes of deep breathing to prepare for sleep.

Take note of how you feel after each type of breathing. Do you find one style more beneficial? How can you use these techniques to help regulate your emotions throughout your day?

SENSORY AWARENESS: ENGAGING THE FIVE SENSES

You're caught in a whirlwind of thoughts. Your mind is racing and jumping from one worry to another. You feel lost in the chaos of it all, and you don't know what to do. Sensory grounding is the life preserver that brings you back to the present by engaging your senses.

This technique is about tuning in to the world around you and using your senses to create a buffer between you and the stressors demanding your attention. By focusing on your senses, you bring yourself back to the here and now, giving your mind the freedom to take a much-needed pause.

1. **SIGHT** - Take a moment to observe the colors and shapes in your environment. Look at the way light dances through a window or the delicate veins of a leaf. Take a moment to people-watch. Sit back and observe the sky, looking for shapes in the clouds above. The simple act of observation can shift your focus from internal chaos to external calm.
2. **TOUCH** - Find something that brings you comfort, like a soft blanket or a smooth stone. Feel its texture under your fingertips, noting the temperature and weight. Let your touch anchor you, reminding you that you are here, safe, and present.
3. **SOUND** - Your ears are another avenue for grounding. Close your eyes and listen to the world around you. It could be the gentle hum of a refrigerator, the rustle of leaves, or the distant chatter of people. Each sound becomes a tether back to the present moment.
4. **SMELL** - This powerful sense is linked closely to memories and emotions. The smell of a fresh cup of coffee or your favorite essential oil can evoke feelings of comfort and safety. Consider purchasing a necklace with a diffuser pendant that you can slip on as needed. It's a discreet way to shift your focus in times of stress.

5. **TASTE** - Try to savor a small piece of food. Pop a breath mint or a piece of dark chocolate into your mouth. Focus on its flavor and texture, and let this simple pleasure root you in the present moment.

One of the greatest strengths of sensory grounding is its versatility. You don't need any special equipment, and you can practice it anywhere. Whether you're on a crowded bus or sitting in your backyard, these techniques are available to you.

During your commute, you might focus on the bumps of the road or the scent of your morning coffee. At home, try creating a sensory retreat by lighting a candle, playing soft music, and wrapping yourself in a cozy blanket or relaxing in a hot bubble bath. These practices remind you that peace isn't a distant destination but something you can cultivate wherever you are.

Sensory grounding helps you manage stress while strengthening your mindfulness. By focusing on your senses, you form a deeper awareness of the present while quieting the noise of anxiety. This purposeful engagement with your surroundings improves your connection to the world, helping you relax and reduce stress.

Consider adding sensory meditation practices to your routine. This practice engages one sense at a time to calm your mind. For example, you might spend a minute or two each morning focusing on the sensation of water running over your hands before you wash your face or the sound of birds singing outside your window. These simple acts of presence can transform ordinary moments into opportunities for grounding and peace.

IMMEDIATE GROUNDING PRACTICES FOR HIGH-STRESS MOMENTS

When life throws us moments of intense stress and everything feels overwhelming and out of control, quick and effective grounding techniques can be a lifeline. One popular method is the 5-4-3-2-1 sensory exercise. In the sensory awareness exercise above, we can choose to focus on one or two of our senses to bring awareness and calm. However, the 5-4-3-2-1 technique calls upon *all* of our senses to anchor us in the present moment when tensions are high.

5. It begins with identifying five things you can see. This can be as simple as the colors around you or the patterns on the floor.

4. Next, notice four things you can physically feel. You might feel the texture of your clothing or the ground beneath your feet. Maybe you find comfort twirling a strand of hair or feeling the steady beat of your pulse on your wrist.

3. Then, find three sounds. Whether it's the hum of a nearby appliance or the distant sound of traffic, listen for those sounds. Yes, even the sound of your breath.

2. Follow with two things you can smell. Perhaps you smell the lingering scent of body wash, your morning coffee, or the fresh air from an open window. Breathe it in.

1. Finally, identify one thing you can taste. It can be as simple as a hint of toothpaste from brushing your teeth.

This exercise can be done anywhere, anytime, making it a powerful tool for grounding when stress hits fast and hard.

Another immediate grounding technique involves movement. When stress levels rise, your body can feel restless and tense. Engaging in simple stretches can help release some of that pent-up energy and tension.

Simple Movement Exercise

- Try stretching your arms overhead, reaching for the sky, and then gently leaning side to side. This motion can open up your chest and shoulders, areas where stress often accumulates.
- Walking is another effective way to ground yourself. Even a short walk around your home or stepping outside for a brief stroll can shift your focus and help regulate your emotions.

Having reliable grounding strategies at your fingertips is essential. When you're deep in the whirlwind of stress, it's easy to forget what works for you. Your personalized grounding toolkit is a collection of your go-to practices that you can rely on when stress levels spike unexpectedly. This could include a list of favorite grounding exercises, a small object that brings you comfort, or even a playlist of calming music. Practicing these techniques regularly ensures they become second nature, ready to be called upon when needed.

To develop your personalized grounding toolkit, experiment with different techniques to see what works best with you. Customize these practices to fit your preferences and lifestyle. Perhaps you find that a combination of sensory exercises and movement works best for you.

Set reminders to practice these techniques, even when you're not stressed, to build familiarity. This routine doesn't have to be rigid. Instead, let it be flexible and adaptable to your needs, evolving as you learn more about what grounds you.

Observation is a key component in refining your grounding practices. After a grounding exercise, take a few moments to notice how you felt before and after. Were there any changes in your stress levels or emotional state? This can give you important feedback on the most effective methods.

As you integrate these grounding practices into your life, you'll find they help in moments of acute stress and contribute to a greater sense of stability and resilience. These techniques are your tools for survival, and your pathways to a future where you can manage stress with confidence and grace.

My Grounding Toolkit

1. Pick three techniques you want to try when you are calm and relaxed.

General Movement   Belly Breathing
Light Stretching   Alternate Nostril
Walking   Breathing
5-4-3-2-1   4-7-8 Breathing
Listening to Music   Box Breathing
Meditation   Other

2. Practice them so they become second nature to you, and you are able to recall them in times of stress. Write your experience below. What did you have success with?

_____

_____

_____

3. What are your top three picks for your grounding toolkit? List them below.

_____

_____

_____

CHAPTER 4
MINDFULNESS AND EMBODIMENT

"It is only when the mind is open and receptive that learning and seeing and change can occur."

— JON KABAT-ZINN

Many cultures and religions believe that the eyes are the windows to the soul. Some have gone so far as to say that the eyes reflect what is happening within a person and what they are feeling. The struggles they are facing. The depths of their emotion. But have you ever taken a moment to see yourself? Not only as a reflection in the mirror, but as a living, breathing being. My guess is that, if you are reading this book right now, you probably recognize that things could be better. And, you would be absolutely correct.

The truth is, as women, we don't often look beyond our bodies to the person within. This is especially true when perimenopause starts to creep in. Our bodies begin to feel foreign to us because we are in a constant state of change. We don't feel like ourselves, but we don't have the time or the energy to stop the world to figure out why. So, we keep going. We keep pushing. And, sometimes, we lose ourselves along the way.

For many, especially those who have faced trauma, the body can feel less like a temple and more like a battlefield. But all is not lost. Mindfulness and embodiment can put you on the winning side of that war. It isn't about being *in* your body; it's about acknowledging all of it. The physical. The emotional. The joy and the pain.

Dissociation is a common response to trauma, and it leaves us feeling completely disconnected from our bodies. It's a survival mechanism that causes us to mentally distance ourselves from overwhelming emotions or sensations. It's an escape of sorts. While it can protect you in the short term, prolonged dissociation keeps you from participating fully in your life.

Embodiment, on the other hand, is about reconnecting with your physical self. As you build awareness of your body's sensations and movements, you engage more deeply with your emotions and experiences, and bring balance to your nervous system.

Body-focused mindfulness exercises encourage you to experience your body in its entirety. Certain yoga poses, such as Mountain Pose or Child's Pose, are great beginner poses. These poses can be practiced with a focus on breath, teaching you to tune into your body's abilities and limits without judgment. A quick search online will give step-by-step instructions and modified versions for those with medical concerns.

Tai Chi and Qi Gong are two traditional Chinese practices that use gentle movements to promote relaxation. This helps to reduce stress and create a sense of calm. Studies have shown that these practices improve mental health by decreasing anxiety and improving emotional stability.

It's like a retreat for the mind. As you progress, you'll notice greater emotional stability, and you'll learn to better guide your feelings...responding rather than reacting to stressors.

These practices don't require a big time commitment, expensive equipment, or diet restrictions. You can seamlessly insert these practices into everyday activities as you see fit. The best part is that you can choose to do something completely different tomorrow, based on the time and energy you have to put toward your practice. Because...life happens.

1. *Mindful walking* is a simple practice that combines your sense of touch with physical movement. Start by focusing on each step, feeling the ground beneath your feet and the rhythm of your breath. This practice teaches you to be fully present, transforming an ordinary walk into a meditative experience.
2. *Conscious eating* is another way to practice embodiment. By savoring the flavor and texture of your meal, you connect with your body's natural cues, promoting a healthier relationship with food.

If you are working to combat emotional eating, try taking a few deep breaths as you sit down for a meal. Check in with your hunger levels before and during the meal to avoid overeating.

These practices force you to slow down and appreciate the richness of sensory experiences, opening a deeper connection with yourself.

> **Embodiment Reflection Exercise**
>
> Take a moment to think about your day. Choose a simple activity like washing your hands or sipping tea. As you engage in this activity, focus entirely on the sensations. Try to notice the warmth of the water or the aroma of the tea.

Embodiment isn't just a practice; it's a way of living that begs you to be present, to listen, and to honor your body's wisdom.

MINDFULNESS MEDITATION FOR EMOTIONAL REGULATION

"I've tried to meditate, but I just can't do it." Sound familiar? What about, "My mind is too busy, and I keep losing focus." Or maybe, "It's boring. I can't sit still that long." These are all common reasons people shy away from meditation. Have you felt this way?

Perhaps the fear of bringing up uncomfortable thoughts kept you from trying in the first place? Some people feel like meditation takes too long to see benefits. Others have a negative association with this type of mental work. But meditation is not meant to be a chore. It's simply a tool that can be used to regulate your emotions.

Imagine sitting quietly with your eyes closed. Now, simply observe your thoughts as they drift into your mind. Before you ask, "How?" or roll your eyes in frustration, keep reading. Instead of trying to completely *quiet* your mind, like most newbies do, try to see what thoughts are pushing forward for your attention.

At first, your thoughts may feel like cars passing on the interstate, fast and furious, and fighting to be in the lead. But you have to remember that you're in control. So, slow things down. Try placing yourself above the rush, like the helicopters that report traffic. See the thoughts. Acknowledge them. Now, let them go. Don't try to process them. Don't try to solve any of the problems. Don't try to block them out. Just breathe and let them pass. Then, return to your breath.

This is mindfulness meditation. At its core, meditation helps you maintain a sense of calm and clarity by increasing self-awareness and reducing your emotional reactivity. When emotions run high, it can feel like you're caught in a storm, with thoughts and feelings swirling uncontrollably. Mindfulness meditation instructs the body to step back and observe the storm without getting swept away.

By practicing non-judgmental awareness, you learn to see your thoughts and emotions without labeling them as good or bad.

This detachment helps you respond to emotions thoughtfully instead of reacting impulsively. Pretty clever, huh?

Numerous studies, including those highlighted by the American Psychological Association, speak to the effectiveness of mindfulness in managing stress and emotional health. Research shows that mindfulness meditation can reduce symptoms of anxiety and depression, support emotional regulation, and even alter brain structures.

Through a process known as neuroplasticity, meditation can stimulate the areas of the brain associated with attention and emotional regulation, giving you more balanced emotional responses.

What the heck is neuroplasticity?

Neuroplasticity is the brain's ability to change and adapt throughout our lives in response to our personal experiences. Crazy right?! This adaptation forms new pathways and connections in the brain. This can work to build up positive functions and replace negative ones, which is why it is so important! It's also incredible for memory issues and those recovering from brain damage due to stroke or injury. It's your brain's way of spring cleaning, but with life-changing benefits.

For many, the idea of starting a meditation practice can feel daunting, but it doesn't have to be. By establishing a routine, you can learn to **be with your body** and hear what it is trying to tell you.

1. One effective mindfulness practice for emotional regulation is *loving-kindness meditation*. This technique focuses on feelings of compassion and love, first towards yourself and then to others. You start by silently repeating phrases like, "May I be happy. May I be healthy. May I be at peace." As you progress, you can direct these wishes towards loved ones, acquaintances, and even those with whom you have conflict. This practice nurtures your sense of empathy, reducing feelings of anger and resentment.
2. As mentioned in Chapter 2, *body scan meditation* is another effective tool for emotional regulation. This type of meditation brings awareness to each part of the body, noticing any tensions or negative sensations. By pairing this with emotional awareness, you can identify how your emotions manifest physically and use that knowledge to bring peace to your emotional state.
3. You can always return to *breath-focused meditation* as a tool to center the rhythm of your breath. Use it as an anchor to bring your wandering mind back to the present, soothing your nervous system into relaxation while reducing anxiety.

Start by setting aside a dedicated time and space for meditation. The space doesn't have to be elaborate; even a quiet corner with a comfortable chair can become your place of refuge. You can sit on the floor, in a chair, or lie down. The important thing is to make yourself as comfortable as possible. I use a meditation pillow that stays in the corner of my office. It helps me sit cross-legged without placing pressure on my ankles, which causes pain and disrupts my practice. I also love to sit outside in a chair when I know I won't be interrupted.

Start with 5 minutes, working your way up as you become more relaxed. Don't worry if you lose focus, shift nervously, get distracted by sounds, or open your eyes. This is normal in the beginning and will get better over time.

Consistency is key, so try to meditate at the same time each day. If your mornings are hectic, you may find it helpful to wake up a few minutes early and practice in the morning to set a peaceful tone for the day. If you have trouble falling asleep or quieting your mind after work, you may want to practice in the evening to unwind. If you are a person who needs some time to get moving in the morning (like me), consider doing a five-minute meditation while still lying in bed. It will help ease your body and mind into the day.

Guided meditation apps can be an excellent tool, especially if you are new to meditation. These structured sessions can be tailored to your needs, which is especially helpful during different times of your life.

If you have never tried meditation or felt like you weren't suited for meditation due to focus issues or lack of knowledge, guided sessions are a lifesaver. Your coach will talk to you throughout the meditation, walking you through next steps, reminding you to relax, and guiding you to the areas where your tension may be stored...taking the pressure off what you **think** you should be doing, and leading the way.

I love guided meditation when my mind is a little too busy for silence. Having someone walk me through my practice is a great way to stay consistent when my regular routine seems out of reach. And, lately I have been using guided meditation at night to help with sleep. Can I just tell you that 99% of the time, I am asleep before the meditation ends. I call that a victory!

Mindfulness meditation encourages you to embrace emotions with curiosity rather than avoidance. This practice is about learning to coexist with your emotions by viewing them as temporary states that ebb and flow.

Important note: If committing to a particular time of day feels daunting, don't let that stop you from developing your practice. It's less important to set a specific time when you will meditate, and more essential to make an effort to practice daily. Think of a time of day when you feel short-fused or anxious, and start your practice there. Meditation shouldn't make you feel more stressed by becoming another item on the to-do list, so give yourself some grace. Just keep moving forward.

SHORT AND EFFECTIVE MINDFULNESS ROUTINES

In our busy lives, finding time for long meditation sessions can seem like an impossible task. However, short meditations are just as effective at achieving positive results while fitting into the most hectic schedules. These quick sessions serve as small yet powerful pauses in your day, helping you reset and re-center. Think of them as little mini retreats amidst the chaos of your day.

Finding a few minutes between meetings or during carpool to engage in a quick mindfulness exercise is a chance to pause and take a mental inventory of your body, noting the areas of tension or anxiety. By doing this, you give yourself a moment to breathe, disconnect from stress, and reconnect with yourself.

Short mindfulness exercises are practical tools that can easily squeeze into your daily routine.

1. One effective method is the *one-minute breathing exercise*. Take sixty seconds and focus solely on your breath. Inhale deeply and release a slow exhale. This simple act can calm the nervous system, help you feel more grounded, and do wonders for your state of mind.
2. Another practice to try is a *short gratitude session*. Spend a few minutes thinking about things you're grateful for. It doesn't have to be big things. Maybe it's the warmth of your morning coffee or the fact that you made it to work on time. Some mornings, I'm grateful for profound things; other mornings, I'm thankful I kept my face in check during that last Zoom call. No lie. The takeaway is that when you focus on gratitude, you shift your mindset from stress and frustration to appreciation.
3. *Mindful stretching* can be a quick way to connect with your body. A few minutes of gentle stretching, while paying attention to your muscles, can release tension and bring you back to the present. These stretches can be done at your desk or in your living room, making this doable no matter where you are. As you stretch, notice how your body feels. Where do you feel the tightness? Where are you at ease? Use this moment as a chance to refresh, recharge, and reset.

The beauty of these practices lies in their effect over time. Consistently engaging in short mindfulness routines can lead to lasting improvements in stress management. Regular use can increase focus and concentration. Before long, you'll be approaching tasks with greater patience and clarity. You might notice your ability to keep calm during challenging times. Like building a muscle, your practice strengthens and equips you to better handle life's ups and downs.

> **"These practices are not one-size-fits-all."**

Experiment with what works best for you. These practices are not one-size-fits-all, so try different exercises. Rotate them daily, weekly, or monthly to keep things fresh and engaging. You might find that some days, a one-minute breathing exercise is just what you need, while other days, a gratitude session fits better. Jot down what you tried, how it made you feel, and any feedback you have.

You can also create a plan of action for the times you need a quick reset or the times you need to devote more energy to your self-care. This intuitive approach is your way of listening to your body's needs while keeping your commitment to yourself.

As we move on, remember that your mindfulness routine is specific to you and you alone. Just like everything we have covered so far, there's no right or wrong way…only what works for you.

CHAPTER 5
CREATIVE EXPRESSION IN SOMATIC THERAPY

"Art speaks where words are unable to explain."

— PAM HOLLAND

Have you ever felt like words aren't enough to express the emotions inside you? It might surprise you to learn that art has a unique way of giving a voice to feelings that might otherwise remain silent. It's a powerful means of self-expression, especially when traditional forms of communication fall short. Creative activities help you tap into a part of yourself that feels intuitive and honest.

Art gives you permission to explore your emotions without the limits of language, providing a space where emotions can flow and find shape through colors, textures, and forms. This kind of expression has nothing to do with skill level or the finished artwork itself; it's about discovery and healing.

The therapeutic rewards of art are well-documented. Engaging with art can reduce stress, serving as a creative outlet that channels emotions into something tangible. The process of creating art can be a form of meditation, bringing you into a state of flow where worries fade and clarity emerges.

As you paint, draw, sculpt, or craft, you may find that your mind becomes quiet. You may notice new thoughts rising to the surface. Thoughts you didn't even know were there. It's possible these thoughts were buried by the noise of daily life. Sit with them for a time. Does it relate to what your body is physically expressing in your artwork? This surfacing of emotions can help you understand your feelings and reactions on a deeper level.

Exploring different artistic mediums can be an exciting side quest. Each medium presents a new and distinct way to engage with your emotions and express your feelings.

1. *Painting or drawing* can be especially powerful for emotional exploration. The act of choosing colors and making marks on a canvas is a way for you to externalize what you're feeling inside. It doesn't matter if you're a talented artist or a beginner; what's important is the act of creating.
2. *Sculpting, needlework, weaving, and jewelry making* are other examples of tactile experiences that can ground you in the present moment. Working with these materials engages your sense of touch, connecting you to the here and now in a very physical way.
3. *Collage-making* is another creative option. This specific method of creative expression brings the different aspects of your life into a cohesive whole. By cutting and arranging different images and textures, you can create a visual story of your experiences and aspirations. This is

particularly helpful for those who struggle to express themselves verbally or in writing. The tactile experience of cutting, arranging, and gluing the pieces of your collage can be therapeutic and calming. If you prefer digital media, creating a screensaver or wallpaper for your smartphone can serve as a reminder of your path and goals.
4. Another exercise to try is *expressive painting sessions*. During these sessions, you paint freely, without judgment or a preferred outcome. It is more about releasing control and letting your emotions guide your brushstrokes.

In my own somatic practice, I've been exploring watercolor therapy. Watercolor therapy is a type of art therapy that encourages emotional expression through watercolor paints. It is relevant to the complex nature of human emotions. The blending and washing of color, along with the building of pigments to create depth, all work to strengthen neuroplasticity and create new pathways in the brain.

I hadn't touched my watercolors since college…many years ago, but I remember the process like it was yesterday. I've always loved the experience of buying art supplies. More specifically, I love paper. My watercolor project called for a 140 lb cold-press, textured page. It came in large sheets that had such a heavy weight. When I selected paper for a project, I felt pressured to produce something of quality…lest I "waste" the page. (Gasp!)

I've always preferred the wet-on-wet technique. The process is exactly how it sounds: you wet the page **before** applying the watercolors. That's when the magic happens. As soon as the color hits the page, the pigment flows out organically, taking a life of its own. It's not ideal for staying "in the lines" like we are often taught as children. It's expressive and freeing, and forces you to think spontaneously as the paint takes a path of its own accord.

But, enough of me geeking out about watercolors. Art therapy isn't about creating perfect artworks; it's about capturing your thoughts and feelings visually. So, use whatever materials inspire you to create. Whether you try pencils, crayons, markers, paints, or start with glueing magazine cutouts, just let your intuition guide you, and don't be afraid to try new things.

> "The value lies in the creation, not the final piece."

As you engage with these exercises, focus on the process rather than the end product. Embrace the imperfections in your artwork as you work through expressing yourself on paper.

Visual Expression Exercise

Set aside time this week to work on visual expression. This exercise isn't about achieving a specific result; it's about the experience of connecting with yourself through art.

- Begin with a blank page and choose a theme or emotion to explore.
- Use colors, shapes, and images that appeal to you, and release yourself to create without overthinking.
- Allow yourself to receive the emotions that arise during this process, and jot down any thoughts around the edges of your page.

When making art as a form of somatic expression, remember that the benefits are in the process of creating, not the final piece. Through this process, you can discover the freedom to express yourself in ways you never considered before.

JOURNALING FOR EMOTIONAL RELEASE AND DISCOVERY

We've touched on journaling in previous chapters, but we'll dig a little deeper here. Journaling can be a great way to access emotions stored within your body. When you put pen to paper, don't think about the words you are writing. Instead, think of each entry as a key to unlocking your subconscious thoughts and feelings that were hidden long ago.

Free writing is, as its name suggests, an anything-goes method where your thoughts simply flow through you without censorship. Think of it like having a conversation with your soul. You can be completely honest and open, which can be incredibly powerful for those dealing with trauma or chronic stress who find it difficult to articulate verbally.

Reflective journaling tracks emotional patterns over time. As you jot down your daily experiences, you may notice recurring themes and triggers by comparing your responses over time. This can reveal a lot as you progress. For instance, you might realize that certain situations consistently evoke anxiety or that specific interactions leave you feeling drained.

This awareness is the first step in developing effective coping strategies. By identifying these patterns, you gain clarity on your triggers and can begin to explore ways to manage them constructively.

If you've ever felt the need to "recharge" after social interactions, reflective journaling can help to reveal the reasons behind those feelings of exhaustion.

To guide you through this exploratory process, see the journaling prompts below. These prompts are designed to help you tap into your emotions and experiences. They serve as starting points, guiding you through the complexities of your inner self.

1. Consider writing about a recent bodily sensation and its associated emotion. What did it feel like? What was happening at the time? This exercise encourages you to make connections between your physical and emotional states.
2. Write about your strengths, accomplishments, or a future vision of you as the best version of yourself. Allow any thoughts, images, or memories to reveal themselves and write them down. Did you notice any movement, warmth, or tingling sensations in your body as you went through the exercise?

Engaging in a regular journaling practice can lead to greater self-understanding and emotional release. As you write consistently, you create a safe space for your thoughts and feelings. This practice can be a cathartic release of emotions that might otherwise remain unspoken.

Over time, journaling can become a form of therapy, providing clarity and peace of mind. By returning to your entries, you can measure progress and gain perspective on your personal growth.

To keep your journaling practice engaging, consider writing a few lines of poetry or drafting a letter to yourself.

Poetry can capture emotions in a unique way, transforming complex feelings into powerful language. Writing letters to your past or future self can bring perspective, compassion, and emotional release. These creative approaches can give momentum to your practice and encourage you to explore your emotions from different angles.

SAMPLE LETTER PROMPTS

- Apologize or ask for forgiveness
- Be honest about something you've hidden
- Share feelings you've been too scared to voice
- Reflect on how a relationship helped you grow
- Say goodbye
- Say thank you
- Make a promise to yourself
- Accept something that has happened
- Let something go

Writing to Heal

1. Use one of the sample letter prompts to draft a letter. If physical writing is difficult, consider typing it in a note on your phone or a blank document on your computer. It's important to note that if the trauma is recent or still overwhelming to you, don't force this process.

2. Consider your safety when writing this letter. In instances of abuse in the home, writing such a letter could be dangerous due to an abusive partner. In these cases, consider writing it during a therapy session or in a public space where you can dispose of it without fear of it being intercepted.

3. Write directly to yourself or the person you are addressing. Be completely honest. Do not attempt to sound formal or different. Write in your natural voice without worrying about spelling or grammar. Do not share this letter with anyone. It is for your eyes only.

4. Read it. Read it to yourself or your therapist. Read it out loud, or silently. Just read it.

5. Burn it. Shred it. Bury it. Have your therapist hold it for future work. Tear it into a million itty, bitty, tiny pieces and discard them in multiple garbage cans throughout the city. Just kidding…Well, maybe not so much. Only you know the effects of the letter being found, so protect your peace by disposing of it properly.

MUSIC AND MOVEMENT: CREATIVE PATHWAYS TO HEALING

Music has a different way of stirring emotions, often reaching places words cannot. Have you ever let a song completely wash over you? Have you felt the rhythm of an instrument syncing with your heartbeat as you sit quietly? Music can evoke a range of emotions, from joy to sorrow and everything in between. It's a powerful tool in your healing journey.

When you listen to music that matches your mood, you give yourself permission to feel and process emotions that might otherwise stay hidden. Subconsciously, it might be why you can't listen to certain music when you are sad, or why a specific song can always raise your spirits. Creating personalized playlists for different moods can be a form of emotional self-care. You might have a playlist that lifts your mood on tough days, or nature sounds that soothe you when anxiety strikes. Each song becomes a thread that weaves through your emotions with comfort and understanding.

Through movement, you can communicate and release what words can't capture. Movement, particularly dance, is a deep form of emotional expression.

Have you ever danced like no one was watching, letting your body move freely, without fear of judgment? That's a form of movement therapy…even if you didn't realize it at that time.

In freeform dance sessions, you are encouraged to use spontaneous movement to release tension and express yourself fluidly, without choreography. It's a space for emotional release. There are no rules. You pick the music. You choose the movement. You reap the benefits.

If freeform dance doesn't suit you, there are structured movement therapies, like **Laban Movement Analysis (LMA)** or **5Rhythms**, that provide a framework. They will take you through a series of movements that encourage emotional release. But, before you jump in, be sure to do your research.

It isn't necessary to pay for a structured movement service, especially in the beginning. You can find several videos on YouTube that will provide some insight into this type of therapy and familiarize you with expression in this format. From there, you can decide if this is something you'd like to pursue further.

Creative Pathway Exercise

- Want to take your practice one step further? Try combining music and movement to create a more integrated healing experience.
- Put on your favorite song and dance.
- Close your eyes and surrender to the music.
- Let your body move organically, as it wishes.
- Notice the sensations in your body and the emotions that arise.
- Give your body permission to release those feelings.
- Remember, this isn't about choreography. Don't worry if the movements feel disconnected. We are focusing on freedom and expression.
- How do you feel? Does your body feel lighter? Do you feel more connected to your inner self?

Expressive movement reaches the body physically and emotionally. Physically, you release pent-up emotions, which reduces stress and tension stored in your muscles. Emotionally, it strengthens your sense of freedom and self-expression, encouraging you to be in your body with confidence and grace.

As you explore the creative pathways of music and movement, remember that these practices are personal and unique to you. There's no right or wrong way to move. So, find what suits you and embrace it completely.

These creative outlets can open paths to healing that you might not have considered before. Keep your mind and heart open to new experiences and the opportunities they provide to connect with your body.

CHAPTER 6
PERSONALIZING SOMATIC EXERCISES

"If it's out of your hands, it deserves freedom from your mind too."

— IVAN NURU

Have you ever tried a new fitness class, only to leave disappointed and feeling like it was a huge waste of time? Maybe you had a bad day, or the exercises felt too intense? Maybe it was just too boring or too slow? Personalizing your somatic practices is like finding the perfect workout. Finding something that works for you is essential to staying on course.

The advantage of personalizing your somatic practice is its flexibility. It's a custom-crafted playbook built according to your goals, needs, and lifestyle. It's a tool meant to fit seamlessly into your daily life, and this chapter is about helping you find that perfect fit.

Like spending time with your favorite person, custom somatic practices are necessary for emotional regulation. Each of us carries different stressors and triggers, and what works for one person may not work for another.

Recognizing the things that cause stress in your life is the first step in building your plan. Is it the rush of your morning commute, family or relationship struggles, an important deadline, or perhaps the quiet of the evening that brings unease? Identifying these personal triggers helps you choose the correct path to counteract them.

Equally important is finding the time of day when you feel most receptive to trying new things. Some people find solace in morning routines that set a positive tone for the day, while others prefer unwinding after the workday or just before bed.

Pinpointing your unique needs can guide you in approaching somatic therapy effectively. Some therapists offer patients a lifestyle assessment questionnaire to help them evaluate their daily schedule, obligations, and energy levels. This provides clarity on when and how to incorporate your plan.

Think about your current routine. Are there moments of downtime that could be transformed into moments of mindfulness? How is your energy? Knowing how your energy fluctuates throughout the day can prepare you for success. Perhaps midmorning is your peak time for focus, making it ideal for breathwork, while afternoons might need a gentle movement break to reinvigorate your spirit. Listening to your body's cues will help you decide the type of somatic action it requires.

Try to familiarize yourself with a variety of somatic exercises, and have a few preferred ones on hand for those unexpected times of need. This ensures that you can choose what fits you best at that moment in time.

- For busy professionals, **quick breathing exercises** like box breathing can be a lifeline amid hectic workdays. These can be done discreetly at your desk, helping you reset and refocus.

- If you're juggling the demands of young children, **simple movement exercises** that include your little ones can be both grounding and bonding. Try turning playtime into a mindful moment, where you and your child stretch and breathe together.

- For frequent travelers, **quick grounding techniques** are more important than frequent-flyer miles. Something as simple as feeling the texture of your seat or focusing on the rhythm of your breath can anchor you during travels, bringing you stability in unfamiliar environments.

Experimentation and flexibility are important to keep your somatic practices engaging and effective. Don't be afraid to try new things, and rotate exercises to prevent monotony.

You might find that what worked last month doesn't quite fit now, and that's okay. Life changes, and our practices should evolve with them. Adapt your routine in response to the shifts in your life, whether it's a new job, challenging family dynamics, or even changing seasons.

Perhaps the outdoor walking meditation you loved in the summer turns into a cozy indoor breathwork session as the winter weather approaches. You can create a sustainable and supportive somatic routine when you align your exercises with your lifestyle.

Somatic Practice Checklist

- Identify Stressors: List three common stress triggers in your life.
- Find Your Time: Note your peak energy times and suitable practice slots.
- Choose Your Practice: Select two somatic exercises to try this week.
- Reflect: After each practice, jot down how you felt before and after.

LOW-ENERGY DAYS: GENTLE SOMATIC APPROACHES

We've all had days when getting out of bed feels like a monumental task. You might wake up and find that your energy is depleted before the day has started, leaving you with a lack of motivation and a sense of fatigue that kills your to-do list.

It's okay to have these days. They are a natural part of life. But, they may come more frequently when dealing with times of excess stress, working on healing past trauma, experiencing symptoms of peri-menopause, or living with chronic illness.

Recognizing and acknowledging how your body feels is the first step towards self-care. Be kind to yourself, and remember that low-energy days do not define your strength *or your worth*. Instead of pushing through to the point of exhaustion, these moments allow you to accept the gift of grace and embrace gentle approaches that honor where you are right now.

Gentle somatic exercises can be especially helpful when energy is scarce. They require minimal effort, but offer a way to stay committed to healing without overextending yourself. We've talked about each of the items listed below, but the purpose of mentioning them here is to think about them from a *low-energy* perspective.

What would these practices look like on those days when your energy is scarce?

BODY SCAN - A seated or lying-down body scan might be exactly what you need. While focusing your attention on different parts of your body, notice any sensations or tensions, and let them soften with each breath. It's a great way to connect with your body without exerting physical energy. Best of all, it can be done from the comfort of your bed or your favorite spot on the sofa.

BREATHWORK - Simple breath awareness exercises are another gentle way to center yourself. By observing your natural breathing rhythm, you can create a sense of calm and presence. This practice doesn't demand much of your body. Your only focus is to rest in the rhythm of your breath, letting go of stress and tension as you exhale.

STRETCHING - Gentle stretching routines can teach you to maintain your connection to your body on low-energy days. These stretches don't have to be intense. A few minutes of stretching your arms overhead, gently twisting your torso, or rolling your shoulders can release accumulated tension. These movements help maintain flexibility and keep your body engaged, even when you're not up for a full workout. The goal is to recognize your limits and honor your body's needs while giving yourself some love and attention…and lots of grace.

Even when energy is limited, gentle practice is a way to stay connected to your body. It's a reminder that healing is a continuous process, even on the days you feel stuck. This level of self-awareness and emotional strength acts as a gentle anchor in your day.

By prioritizing gentle movement and breathwork, you create a space of safety and comfort when everything else feels overwhelming. Consistency on low-energy days is an expression of self-love that reiterates your commitment to self-care.

Setting realistic goals and expectations should include options for gentle practice days. These pre-planned days can encourage you to keep going when you feel overwhelmed. Healing isn't always about grand gestures. Sometimes the smallest acts of self-care have the most impact.

CREATING A PERSONALIZED SOMATIC ROUTINE

Before building your personal routine, consider how often and how long you'd like to practice. Frequency and duration are important factors in creating a routine that doesn't feel overwhelming.

You might begin with daily sessions or decide to practice three times a week. See what feels right for you. Some may prefer short, frequent practices, while others might relish in longer, more immersive sessions. The key is finding a balance that is comfortable but provides enough challenge to keep you engaged.

Try mixing different types of exercises that complement each other. If you include activities that stretch you physically or emotionally, you should also consider adding things that bring you comfort.

> ***HINT:*** Don't be afraid to change things up if your regular practice feels "off" on certain days. If you wake up needing a different path, pivot and do what is necessary. It is better to be consistent with practice than to skip a day because your schedule feels less manageable.

A well-structured routine will soon become second nature. Before long, you'll integrate your somatic exercises into existing habits to make them part of your daily flow. Try pairing a short breathing exercise with your morning coffee. Or, while engaging in a gentle movement practice before bedtime, you might mentally explore what you are grateful for that day.

If you're a planner girlie, you already know that using checklists or trackers can be an effective way to view your progress and maintain accountability. There's something deeply satisfying when you tick off tasks that bring you a sense of accomplishment and motivation.

And, if you're not a planner girlie, that's okay too. Over time, your routine will evolve to mirror the changes in your life as you grow. Regular self-assessments will help you identify what's working and what you need to adjust.

Continue asking yourself how each practice makes you feel and whether it aligns with your current needs and goals. As you grow more confident in your abilities, you might incorporate new exercises or increase the intensity of your existing routine. This adaptability keeps your practice flexible, meeting you wherever you are.

Your somatic routine is a living, breathing entity that grows with you. Your needs will change, and so will your practice. Embrace this fluidity and adjust your routine to support your personal needs.

My Low Energy Plan

How can you incorporate somatic practices on the days when energy is scarce?

_____

_____

_____

Over time, try the items listed below and give them a rating based on how you felt before and after. These ratings can be a huge help when you are low on energy and only have the capacity to engage in one or two exercises.

EXERCISE	BEFORE	AFTER
Centering Breath:	1 2 3 4 5	1 2 3 4 5
Pelvic Tilt:	1 2 3 4 5	1 2 3 4 5
Cat-Cow Stretch:	1 2 3 4 5	1 2 3 4 5
Shoulder Rolls:	1 2 3 4 5	1 2 3 4 5
Hip Circles:	1 2 3 4 5	1 2 3 4 5
Overhead Stretch:	1 2 3 4 5	1 2 3 4 5
Body Scan Relaxation:	1 2 3 4 5	1 2 3 4 5

CHAPTER 7
BUILDING EMOTIONAL RESILIENCE

"The greater the wounding, the more numerous and powerful our protectors need to be."

— BONNIE BADENOCH

Can you recall a moment when a comment or situation caused your body to visibly react? Did your heart start racing, or did your palms begin to sweat? Maybe you noticed your muscles tense up?

Personally, this is an easy yes for me. Quite honestly, there are too many instances to count. These responses, often involuntary and intense, are identified as emotional triggers.

Triggers are specific stimuli that start an emotional reaction within us. They are like hidden landmines, ready to explode when we least expect them, impacting our thoughts and behaviors.

A harsh word from a close friend, a critical remark from a colleague, or the unexpected reminder of a past trauma can set off emotions that can leave us feeling vulnerable and sometimes spiraling out of control. They dictate how we react to the world, influencing our relationships and sabotaging our happiness.

Emotional triggers are deeply personal. What triggers one person might not affect another, even if they experienced the same trauma. Often, these triggers stem from unresolved issues or past experiences.

Confrontation is a common trigger, stirring feelings of anxiety or anger. Criticism, whether constructive or not, can evoke feelings of inadequacy or defensiveness. And reminders of past trauma, even subtle ones, can force us into overwhelming emotions.

These triggers engage the brain's limbic system. This part of the brain is responsible for processing emotions and memories. It can cause physical responses like increased heart rate and sweating, as if our bodies are sounding an alarm to signal danger… even when the threat is no longer present.

Identifying personal triggers requires vulnerability. Take note of the situations that evoke strong emotional reactions and the thoughts and physical sensations accompanying them.

Emotional Trigger Exercise

Consider moments in your life when you felt particularly emotional or reactive. These memories can provide clues into the origins of your triggers, helping you understand why certain situations provoke such intense responses.

- Identify the moment: _____

   _____

- What was said or done? _____

   _____

- How did it make you feel? _____

   _____

- What thoughts did it bring up? _____

   _____

Our past experiences play a significant role in shaping our emotional responses. Childhood memories, in particular, can leave lasting impressions that influence how we perceive and react to the world. If you were frequently criticized as a child, you might react defensively to criticism as an adult, even when it is well-intentioned.

Learned behaviors from early experiences often become deeply rooted patterns that we carry into adulthood. Over time, these patterns can strengthen emotional triggers, making them seem like automatic responses. When we are able to recognize the link between past experiences and current triggers, we can start to unravel these patterns and find new ways to respond.

Reframing emotional responses is a powerful technique for altering how you identify and react to triggers. Cognitive restructuring, a component of Cognitive Behavioral Therapy (CBT), is very effective in this reframing technique. It prompts you to challenge and modify negative or irrational thoughts that arise during triggering situations.

Let's explore this a little further with the example below.

Remember that story I told you in Chapter 1 about the runaway baby gate? Yeah, how could you forget? As a quick recap, a simple look from my husband, accompanied by a little disapproving head shake, had me thinking my 31-year marriage was in jeopardy. Wow.

It's a gigantic leap to go from accidentally sending a baby gate sailing down a flight of stairs straight into divorce court, but let's unpack that a bit by looking at a few methods I can use to combat my triggering thoughts.

1. *Socratic Questioning* teaches you to challenge those triggering thoughts by asking logical follow-up questions like, "Has my husband ever expressed the desire for a divorce?" Or, "If the roles were reversed, would I be considering divorce as a resolution?" I can go even further by asking, "What is a more realistic way to look at this?"

2. *Decatastrophizing* is where you purposely go deeper into the rabbit hole to explore the worst-case scenario, and then look at how that would impact you. I might ask, "If he was upset enough to consider leaving, what would happen next?" I'd like to think we would end up in couples therapy, or maybe he would suggest

that I see a doctor. Can you see how the story that I tell myself is changing? This type of questioning helps you shift from panic mode into problem-solving.

3. **Nonjudgmental Awareness** asks us to look at the thoughts and feelings surrounding this situation without attaching any meaning or judgment to them. I might sit with that feeling of guilt and shame and ask myself, "Where do I feel that in my body?" Once I identify it, I might ask, "Can I sit with this feeling of shame and breathe through the discomfort it brings, without reacting to it?"

Learning to reframe emotional responses when faced with triggers is a big step toward creating resilience and emotional stability. Remember that you are not your thoughts, so don't believe every thought that enters your brain.

Journal Prompts

- "Describe a recent situation that triggered a strong emotional response. What thoughts and physical sensations did you experience?"

- "Can you pinpoint a time from your past that might be linked to this trigger. How did it shape your current reaction?"

- "Choose a triggering thought and challenge its realism. What evidence supports or contradicts it?"

Note: Don't overwhelm yourself with the journaling process. Beautiful notebooks are obviously welcome, but don't forget that your cell phone is very capable of capturing your thoughts. Creating notes on your cell phone is a great way to jot down things as they happen, and your memory is fresh. You may want to add details once you've had time to process things, or delete the note completely. It's entirely up to you how you decide to journal, but remember that it can be as simple, as organized, or as pretty as you like.

TECHNIQUES FOR BUILDING RESILIENCE

Emotional resilience gives you the adaptability to bend without breaking in the face of stress. Picture resilience as a sturdy tree in a windstorm, flexible but firmly grounded. Emotional resilience provides that kind of stability during life's storms.

When challenges arise, it keeps you moving with a steady heart and clear mind. It doesn't mean you won't feel stress or sadness, but you'll have the tools to manage those feelings and keep moving forward.

One quick method to build emotional resilience is gratitude journaling. This type of journaling is fast and easy. You simply note two or three things you're thankful for at some point in your day. This teaches your mind to shift your focus from what's wrong to what's right.

Don't get caught up on the big things. Even on the toughest days, finding small blessings like a warm cup of tea or a compliment from a stranger can change your perspective.

Before bed, I like to list three things that I am grateful for from that day. It may only be a few short words if I'm tired, but I don't pressure myself to write more. It really helps me relax before going to sleep."

— E. K.

Gratitude journaling can rewire your brain to *recognize* positivity, which strengthens your emotional resilience. It's up to you to determine how simple or structured you want it to be. Paper journals have been a common way to start, but there are also many smartphone apps to track gratitude. You may decide that typing a note on your phone or recording a voice memo is the easiest way to stay consistent. It doesn't matter how it's done, as long as you keep doing it.

Gratitude Journaling Exercise

What part of the day would gratitude journaling work best for you? Is there a time of day that is tougher for you to remain positive? How can gratitude journaling help with this? Write five things that you are grateful for in the space below.

1. _____
2. _____
3. _____
4. _____
5. _____

Visualization techniques are another powerful tool used to create positive images in the mind. When we intentionally choose to envision a peaceful life where we are healed and safe, we actively work to change the negative images and memories we might be carrying.

Try to spend a few minutes each day visualizing yourself successfully overcoming future challenges. Picture the steps you'll take to get there, and the feelings of accomplishment you'll experience when it is completed. This is a mental rehearsal, of sorts, that prepares you to face any difficulties with confidence.

The universe is dying for you to be kind to yourself.

— DR. MARTHA BECK, PHD

I recently saw an interview with Dr. Martha Beck, PhD, on social media. For those who don't know her, Dr. Beck is a sociologist and world-renowned coach with three Harvard degrees and an ongoing library of bestselling books. In the interview, she said something that caught my attention. "The universe is dying for you to be kind to yourself." I literally gasped when I heard those words leave her mouth. I backed it up so I could listen again, and again, and again.

How many times are we truly kind to ourselves? Better yet, how often are we kind to ourselves in the way we aim to be kind to others? My guess is rare to never. One of the first ways to begin being kind to yourself is to start speaking kindly to yourself.

Positive self-talk is the inner dialogue that encourages and lifts you up when you're down. It's not something you might think about on a daily basis, but it is so crucial in your healing journey.

Affirmations can be a vessel to get you to that place of self-care. Simply explained, affirmations are positive statements about yourself that are recited regularly to nurture and support you along the way.

Try starting your day with a handful of affirmations like, "I am strong," or "I can handle whatever comes my way." You can also add one of Dr. Beck's recommended affirmations, "I am meant to live in peace." I love that one.

So often, we trust whatever thought enters our brain and treat it as canon. But we are not meant to believe everything we think. When negative thoughts creep in, challenge them. Ask yourself if they're based on facts, fears, or assumptions. This rational questioning helps dismantle irrational fears and boosts your confidence. Over time, this positive internal dialogue can transform how you perceive and respond to life's ups and downs.

Below are a few of my favorite affirmations. I find it therapeutic to recite these in front of a mirror. I look myself in the eyes, and I speak to myself in the same loving tone I would use with a treasured friend.

- I am loved. I am whole. I am worthy. I am ENOUGH.
- Today, I choose progress over perfection.
- I release the need to be perfect.
- I trust in my abilities to achieve my goals.
- I deserve all the good things that come my way.
- I am grateful for my life and those in it.
- Every small step moves me toward my goals.
- I am meant to live in peace.

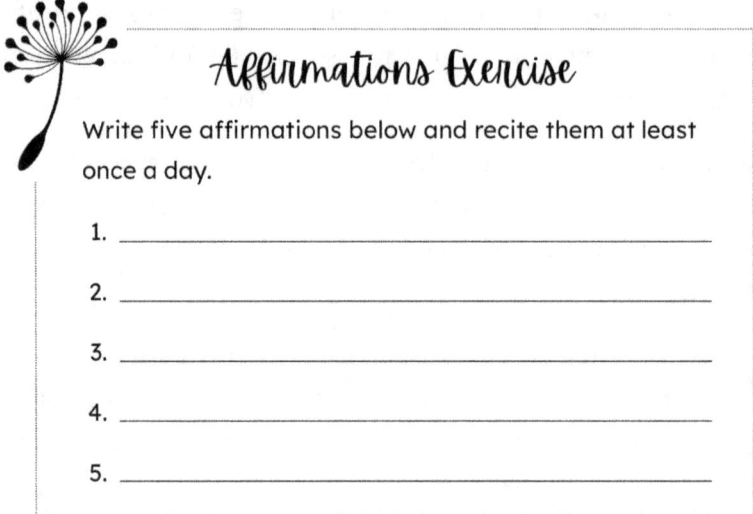

Affirmations Exercise

Write five affirmations below and recite them at least once a day.

1. _____
2. _____
3. _____
4. _____
5. _____

Another must-have on this path to healing is having a support network. No one is an island; having people to lean on can make all the difference. Start by naming a few supportive friends and family members who have been a source of encouragement and understanding. These are individuals you trust to provide a listening ear or a comforting presence when you need it most.

Engaging in community groups or group therapy sessions can also be beneficial. Whether you attend a local meetup or an online forum, these spaces can become places of connection and shared experiences. Participating in group activities or therapy sessions can provide new perspectives and coping strategies to add to your personalized emotional toolkit.

> ### My Support Team
>
> Write down the names of three people you can reach out to for encouragement.
>
> 1. _____
> 2. _____
> 3. _____

Note: Sometimes, past experiences make trust difficult. If this feels uncomfortable right now, skip this exercise. Work toward building trust with one person and come back to this when the time is right.

Building resilience isn't about never falling down; it's about getting back up and trying again...and again. Most importantly, it's about remembering to get up with a little more wisdom and strength each time. You are strong, so believe in yourself.

SELF-REGULATION: MANAGING EMOTIONAL REACTIONS

You know those days when everything seems to go off track. Your morning coffee spills, traffic is a nightmare, your little one refuses to put on shoes, and by the time you reach your destination, your nerves are frayed.

It's moments like these where the ability to self-regulate becomes essential. Okay…but what exactly is self-regulation? I'm glad you asked.

Self-regulation is the ability to manage your emotions, thoughts, and reactions to keep a sense of balance in your daily life. It's like having an internal compass that guides you back to calmness when you can feel the chaos creeping in. Pretty sweet, right?

This prevents emotional outbursts, which can put an unwanted strain on relationships and exacerbate stress. It also sharpens your focus and decision-making abilities by keeping you grounded and clear-headed, even in times of turmoil. It's a win-win!

The art of self-regulation isn't about suppressing emotions; it's about understanding and guiding them effectively. In Chapter 2, we learned how progressive muscle relaxation can aid in reducing stress. The tensing and slow release of each muscle group helps you let go of tension and leaves you feeling more at ease. It calms the body and signals your mind to slow down.

Another powerful tool is mindful breathing, which acts as a quick reset button for your emotions. Whenever you feel overwhelmed, try taking a few deep breaths, focusing on the sensation of air entering and leaving your lungs. This simple act can help soothe immediate reactions, bringing you back to the present moment to formulate a more measured response.

Self-regulation is closely tied to your health. By managing your emotional reactions, you can reduce symptoms of anxiety and depression. This leads to healthier relationships as you become better at communicating your needs and understanding the needs of others.

We've all experienced an uncomfortable conversation with a friend that might have caused us to automatically react defensively. With self-regulation, you can press the pause button, breathe, and then respond thoughtfully. This intentional pause before reacting reinforces trust in your relationship and shows mutual respect.

Your ability to self-regulate also improves your decision-making skills. When you're not clouded by intense emotions, you can assess situations more clearly and make informed choices or actions that align with your values and goals.

You might be thinking, "But, how?" Keep reading, my friend.

Setting daily goals for emotional check-ins can help you stay attuned to your feelings and reactions. Take a few minutes each day to check in on your emotional state, asking yourself what you're feeling and why. This self-awareness practice can help you address any emotional spikes before they escalate.

Utilizing apps or resources to track your progress can also be beneficial. Many mindfulness and meditation apps have guided practices and reminders, helping you stay committed to your self-regulation goals.

No matter how you incorporate self-regulation techniques into your routine, you'll lay the foundation for emotional stability and resilience. You become more attuned to your reactions and learn to maneuver through life's challenges gracefully and confidently.

CHAPTER 8
INTEGRATING SOMATIC THERAPY INTO DAILY LIFE

"The only way out is through."

— ROBERT FROST

Do you dream of starting your day with a sense of calm and purpose? No scrambling to get ready while your mind takes you on a downward spiral of the day's responsibilities. Impossible? Not with a morning ritual. I know. I know. You think, "But I'm not a morning person." Well, same. But morning rituals help to set the tone for your entire day.

A few minor adjustments at the start of your day can make a recognizable difference in how you approach the hours ahead. Beginning your day with intention helps align your mental and emotional state.

A structured morning routine is more than ticking off a list of tasks; it's a way to build mental clarity and focus. When you wake up with a plan, you start your day with a sense of purpose and goals that guide you. Whether you're choosing to be more patient, more productive, or simply more present, these intentions act as a compass, directing your actions and thoughts throughout the day.

My day starts with my faith. Each day, I choose a scripture to focus on, grateful for another day to make a difference.

Movement is next. Each morning, I have a specific routine, but EVERY day involves a 1-mile walk with my husband. We rarely miss a morning. We may have conversations of what the day ahead has in store for each of us, or what happened yesterday. Sometimes we talk about our grandsons and how much we love them. Other days, we walk in quiet, appreciating simply being together before we begin our day.

My daily routine helps to anchor me in my faith and reminds me that what I do is part of a bigger plan. The exercise helps my mind slow down and gives me increased focus and energy. It also allows me time to listen to scripture and set my day up for good things.

I want to be a positive example for those around me, so it's up to me as to how that example will look. I use it wisely. And for these days, I am thankful and blessed.

— SHEILA

Incorporating simple somatic exercises like gentle stretching or yoga sequences helps to awaken your body, releasing tension and stimulating your senses. One example is a gentle forward bend paired with a few deep breaths. As you feel the stretch in your back and the grounding of your feet, you prepare your body and mind for the day ahead.

Not feeling up to movement first thing in the morning? No problem. Breath awareness exercises are equally as powerful and help to center your thoughts while connecting with your body's rhythm. Focusing on deep, intentional breathing can calm your mind and set a peaceful tone for the day.

Creating a personalized morning ritual allows you to tailor your time to suit your lifestyle and needs.

Perhaps you start by mindfully preparing tea or coffee, savoring the aroma and warmth as a form of meditation. This small ritual can become a cherished moment of stillness before the demands of your day kick in.

You may also decide to set a daily intention in your journal. You can jot down a few thoughts or goals for the day and visualize what you hope to achieve or feel. This practice identifies your priorities while reinforcing your commitment to personal growth and prosperity.

CONSISTENCY IS KEY!

Yes, I know…I sound like a broken record, but consistency is so important. Don't get me wrong here. I'm not talking about consistency in the length of your morning routine, or the intensity at which you exercise, and I certainly don't care how detailed your journal entries are. The important thing is doing it. Over and over and over and over so that your brain *recognizes the pattern*, and it becomes easier to repeat moving forward.

This brings us back to neuroplasticity…remember that word? Your brain is hardwired to look for patterns within your life. It creates new neural pathways when it sees a behavior repeated consistently. The more consistent you are, the stronger the neural pathways become, and the more automatic the behavior can be. Pretty cool, right?

So, use your phone for reminders or alarms, and put that sticky note on the bathroom mirror. It might feel a little forced in the beginning, but we're thinking about the big picture.

When I envision those new pathways opening up in my brain, it feels like I'm forging my own path forward. It helps me visualize myself breaking free of the things in my past that I could not personally control at that time.

Morning Ritual Checklist

- Stretch Sequence: Develop a five-minute stretching routine to engage your body.
- Breath Focus: Spend three minutes on breath awareness to center your mind.
- Mindful Moment: Enjoy your morning beverage mindfully, focusing on the experience.
- Journal Reflection: Write down one intention or goal for the day in your journal.

Can your morning routine use a little shake-up? You'd be surprised how a few simple adjustments can impact the flow of your day. Take a moment each evening to consider how your morning practices shaped your day. How can you adjust your routine tomorrow morning to better support your goals? The beauty is in the details, so make it work *for* you.

MINDFUL BREAKS: INCORPORATING SOMATIC MOMENTS AT WORK

In the hustle of a busy workday, we often forget to pause. It's easy to get caught up in the momentum, pushing through without a moment's rest. But don't underestimate the benefits of mindful breaks throughout your day. A couple of minutes of intentional focus can make all the difference for your productivity.

Now, hold on…I'm not talking about stepping away from your desk to hide in a bathroom. No judgment; I've been there before. But I want you to seek out ways to *refresh* your mind and body.

Find the moments that renew your spirit and awaken your senses. These little breaks can prevent burnout caused by prolonged stress. They give your mind a chance to reset and allow you to return to your tasks with renewed energy and clarity.

Use this time to work on your somatic practice. Start with simple desk stretches. These gentle movements can release built-up tension from sitting for long periods.

> ### Desk Stretch
> Reach your arms overhead, stretching your back, and alternate raising one arm higher than the other. Bring your arms down and try rolling your shoulders. Roll them forward and backward for about 30 seconds each.

These stretches ease physical tension and invigorate your mind. And, if you're really feeling productive, combine stretching with a breathing exercise for immediate relaxation. Just a few deep breaths can calm your nervous system, reducing stress and anxiety.

Quick visualization techniques can also be effective. Close your eyes for a moment and imagine a peaceful place. Remember your safe space from Chapter 2? Try placing yourself in this area of peace and recalling the things that ignited your senses. Was it a feeling or a particular smell? Perhaps it was a sound, or the lack of sound, that sticks out in your memory.

> ### Breathing Break
>
> If you're comfortable doing so, sit up straight and close your eyes. Inhale deeply through your nose and hold that breath for a second or two. Then release the breath slowly and evenly. Repeat this a few times and pay attention to the shift in your body.

Scheduling these breaks might seem challenging initially, but with a bit of planning, they can seamlessly fit into your day. Not into alarms or sticky notes? Download a free productivity app. There are several out there that help you plan daily, weekly, or monthly goals. These small nudges can help you remember to take a moment for yourself, even on the busiest days.

If you thrive on routine, designate specific times for somatic moments, such as mid-morning and mid-afternoon breaks. These scheduled pauses ensure you take a step back, claiming a moment of peace in your workday.

When stress levels rise, having the proper tools to ground yourself can help you maintain emotional control, even when external demands are high, and build a healthy work-life balance.

Merging somatic moments into your workday is about making the most of your time, so don't stress about finding "extra" time. These practices only require a few mindful minutes and have the ability to transform your day.

EVENING PRACTICES FOR REST AND REFLECTION

As the sun sets and the day winds down, our bodies and minds crave a downward shift from the hustle of the day to a more serene and calming night. Evening reflection can serve as the bridge that guides us from our busy day into a tranquil night. This transition gives your body permission to rest and is necessary for proper mental health.

Creating a peaceful evening environment is a great starting point. Consider dimming the lights, playing soft music, or lighting a candle. These things signal your mind and body that it's time to relax and unwind.

To support this transition, try incorporating some somatic exercises to help ease you into a state of calm.

1. In Chapter 2, we discussed *progressive relaxation*. This simple yet powerful technique involves tensing and slowly releasing each muscle group in your body. This practice relaxes your muscles while calming your mind, promoting a sense of peace and readiness for sleep. Begin at your toes and work your way up to your head. Focus on your breathing as you feel the day's tension melt away.

2. **Gentle evening yoga** or stretching routines are another option. These movements help your body settle into a more restful state by releasing stored tension. A few minutes of stretching can make a big difference, easing you into the night with comfort and peace. YouTube is a great resource for beginners. Look for a 5-10 minute video to start. Over time, you will find specific stretches or poses that make you feel good, and you can add them to your personalized evening flow. One of my favorite evening practices is Yin Yoga. It is the perfect way to put your mind and body in a state of rest before retiring to bed.

3. **Journaling** at the end of the day allows you to keep a tangible record of what went right or wrong, and allows you to process thoughts and emotions to clear your mind before sleep. Open-ended prompts can also guide your journaling. Consider questions like, "What went well today?" or "What did I learn about myself?" These prompts provide a starting point for you to assess your daily experiences and provide feedback for your actions, guiding your choices moving forward.

Maintaining consistent evening practices can also aid in your sleep quality. When you establish a regular bedtime routine, you train your body to recognize when it's time to wind down, developing positive sleep patterns and reducing insomnia. These routines ground you in habits that rejuvenate your body and mind.

You'll likely notice an improvement in your emotional balance as well. Take a few moments each evening to focus on self-care and reflection. This intentional slowing down brings peace to the end of your day and sets the stage for restful sleep.

As you weave these evening practices into your life, remember that they are more than just routines; they are acts of self-care. Take these moments to nurture your body and mind, reconnect with yourself, and prepare for the new day.

CHAPTER 9
CREATIVITY AS A THERAPEUTIC TOOL

"It's not about being good at creativity, it's about creativity being good for you."

— JAMES MCCRAE

Remember when you were a child, immersed in play, lost in imagination, and the world felt limitless. Creativity was a huge part of your language. In all honesty, it's still a huge part of mine. I'm much more at ease when I'm working creatively and independently in my office with a good playlist on my Bluetooth speaker. But, I digress.

Now, imagine harnessing that same unfiltered expression to help heal your emotions. Rediscovering creative arts as a means to explore your feelings is highly beneficial to those with memories too complex or painful to articulate verbally.

Art therapy, as highlighted by the American Art Therapy Association, provides a space where color and form become your voice. It's a space where you are welcome to express emotions and experiences in a safe environment that is free of judgment. This process can help you process trauma and discover more about yourself.

One of the beautiful aspects of art is its ability to convey what words cannot. Colors can mirror your mood, shapes can symbolize experiences or emotions, and your canvas is there to capture whatever emerges. No judgment.

A swirling blue might evoke a feeling of calmness, while jagged red lines might capture moments of anger or chaos. You may choose to focus on one event at a time, or you could decide to use an art journal as a way to visually represent your day.

Using art as a therapeutic practice is a way to externalize your feelings. This artistic release of trapped or suppressed emotions can provide significant relief and understanding. We are not trying to create an artistic masterpiece. We are exploring self-expression. Art becomes a channel for healing, a place where you can be vulnerable and honest with yourself.

I'M NOT ARTISTIC. WHAT CAN I DO?

There are many ways to begin exploring art therapeutically. For those with creative brains, this is your haven, and you may already be utilizing art as therapy. But, for the rest of the population, creativity may not come as easily as expected. Having a variety of ways to make art therapy seem like a viable option starts with a creative path that interests you.

Creative therapy is extensive and ever-growing, so there are infinite possibilities to approach this type of expression. Below are a few simple options we touched on in Chapter 5. Let's see how we can use these options to jumpstart your exploration with art therapy.

1. ***Collage and scrapbooking*** are used to visualize your personal story. Gather images, words, and textures that speak to you, and arrange them on a poster board or a sheet of paper. You can use magazines, cereal boxes, product labels, and more. You may decide to fill in some areas with written quotes or doodles. This exercise helps you see your story from a different perspective, revealing connections and patterns you might not have seen before. If you prefer the digital world, take it to the computer. You may find it therapeutic to keep as a work in progress, adding to it as your somatic practice evolves.

2. ***Abstract painting*** is a wonderful way to release emotions. Allow yourself to paint freely, without a plan or expectation. Try to visualize your emotions as colors, then use those colors to express how you feel in the moment. You may find that different emotions lead you to use different brush strokes, or affect the thickness of the paint you apply to the canvas. The important thing is to let the paint flow, capturing your raw emotions as they pass through you.

3. ***Sculpting, needlework, and other crafting techniques*** are tactile experiences that can ground you in the present. As your hands work with the physical materials, you might find it soothing and meditative, connecting you with your body and helping to regulate any negative emotions. It also serves as an outlet to release emotions tied to experiences that are difficult to put into words. Sculpting is often used to provide a sense of control over emotions associated with experiences that might have previously felt uncontrollable.

These are, by no means, the only ways to incorporate art as therapy. A simple online search can generate many creative alternatives based on your interests and skills. Seems intimidating? Try an adult coloring book. Don't be afraid to step out of your comfort zone. You'll never know how therapeutic something can be until you find the thing that identifies with you.

Expressing your creative process is an integral part of art therapy. As you engage with different art forms, notice any feelings that might arise as you work with colors, shapes, or textures. How does the act of creating influence your mood or perspective? These little bits of feedback can provide a window into your emotional state and the themes present in your life.

Art therapy has really helped me cope with being away from home. I travel a lot for work. So, when I drive, I take my collage and scrapbooking supplies with me.

I use a monthly planning calendar to pencil in all my plans, motivational quotes, thoughts, prayers, and any appointments I have that month. Then, I go back and decorate everything with markers, stickers, washi tape, doodles, and photos that I print on my little travel printer.

The act of arranging everything on the page helps to calm any anxiety I might be feeling and makes me feel more connected to my family while I am away. Seeing the finished work gives me a sense of completion that calms my mind and brings me peace, comfort, and joy during a generally stressful time.

— B.K.M.

EXPLORING MOVEMENT AND DANCE THERAPY

You might not have considered dance or movement as forms of therapeutic somatic expression, but dance is a physical way to communicate emotions without the use of words. In a room filled with music, dance becomes a form of storytelling. Each step and each gesture narrates a part of your story. It's a way to connect with your body, to feel grounded yet free, and to release tensions that have perhaps been stored for far too long.

With movement, you can explore your emotions in a safe and dynamic way, transforming the energy of your feelings into something physical and freeing. Whether it's a gentle sway or a vigorous stomp, each movement is an opportunity to explore and express what's inside.

Structured movement exercises can provide a framework for this exploration. These guided movements, focusing on flow and rhythm, help you tune into your body's natural movements. These sequences flow with the music, gently encouraging you to express emotions that might be difficult to articulate.

On the other hand, improvisational dance is a more spontaneous form of expression. There are no rules or expectations here, just the freedom to move as you feel. It's more about letting your body lead as you follow its wisdom and trust that each movement is precisely what you need.

Movement therapy, including regular movement and dance, can significantly improve mood, reduce anxiety, and create better self-awareness. In movement, you become more attuned to your body's signals, learning to recognize and respond to emotional cues.

This heightened awareness can increase body confidence and self-esteem, as you begin to appreciate your body's ability to express and adapt.

The physical release that comes with movement also reduces stress-related symptoms, helping you release pent-up tension and find a sense of calm. Movement therapy provides a full-bodied approach to health and wellness, integrating physical, emotional, and mental health in a rhythmic dance.

In a group setting, the energy becomes visible, creating a supportive environment where everyone shares a common goal... healing through movement. Participating in group dance therapy sessions can be a powerful way to connect with others on a deep, emotional level. Observing and learning from others' movements can inspire your creative exploration.

In these sessions, you are not alone; you are part of a community that understands and supports you. The collective energy amplifies the therapeutic results, leaving you with validation and belonging. Group dance therapy becomes a space where vulnerability is met with empathy, and each movement is a step towards healing.

WRITING AS A THERAPEUTIC JOURNEY

I recently saw a trend on social media where creators were writing content titled, *"I met my younger self for coffee."* The trend went viral, and soon the world connected over stories of resilience, strength, success, and even unanswered prayers. Total strangers shared personal pieces of their life stories, often reassuring their younger selves that things will be okay...even if it didn't seem that way at the time.

The vulnerability and transparency expressed in their stories opened doors for others to share supportive thoughts and well wishes. It was a personal healing exercise, but when it was shared with the public on social media, it became a group therapy session.

The impact was profound. Those who were vulnerable and shared their stories got support and validation from the online community while encouraging others to be vulnerable, extending this healing exercise to those far beyond their physical reach. That is the power of writing.

Think of writing as an open invitation for thoughts and emotions to flow freely, uninhibited by the need for eloquence or judgment. It's an intimate conversation with yourself...a tool for self-discovery and healing. Through writing, you can peel back another layer of your "emotional onion" and gain clarity on complex feelings.

Freewriting is a stream-of-consciousness exercise in which words spill onto the page without censorship. This practice can uncover emotions that might be lurking beneath the surface. By simply letting things unfold on paper, you may find yourself expressing things that surprise and enlighten you. This can be a great addition to your morning routine. Personally, I prefer this as a way to brain dump before bed, clearing the mind to encourage peaceful sleep.

Structured writing, on the other hand, provides a framework for organizing thoughts, helping you sift through emotions and gain perspective on your experiences. This writing style generally starts with a pre-determined writing prompt. You can find several online, and we will explore that further at the end of the chapter.

Poetry writing is a more abstract and creative outlet for expressing emotions. Through rhythm and metaphor, poetry can capture the essence of your feelings in ways that prose sometimes cannot. This exercise encourages you to explore your inner world, transforming emotions into words that heal.

WRITING EXERCISE IDEAS

Let's visualize for a minute. You sit down in a comfy chair, in a quiet corner. You've got a notebook in hand and a few writing tools ready. You might have a cup of hot tea or relaxing music playing in your earbuds. And, you're ready to explore your mind.

1. To guide your writing process, consider engaging in exercises encouraging you to look within. Writing a letter to your past self can be a powerful act of healing and closure. It empowers you to acknowledge past struggles while giving yourself the compassion and forgiveness you might not have received at that time. As you write, you might find a sense of release, freeing yourself from the weight of past regrets. Allow yourself to feel those things while reminding yourself that you are okay in this moment.

2. Crafting personal narratives is another beneficial exercise. In this exercise, you reframe traumatic experiences into stories of resilience and growth. By taking control of your narrative, you can shift your perspective and claim power over a negative memory, breaking through the victim status.

Writing Prompts

Create a set of writing prompt cards to draw from when you need inspiration.

Include prompts like "Write a letter to your future self" or "Describe a place where you feel completely at peace."

Use these cards as starting points for your writing sessions, encouraging exploration and creativity.

Maintaining a regular writing practice can be another form of therapy. As we've discussed in previous chapters, consistently engaging with your thoughts and feelings helps you develop a deeper understanding of what drives your emotions.

Writing helps to identify patterns, reveal triggers, and highlight progress over time. When you review your entries, in six months or even a year, you'll notice the shift. In turn, this deep sense of accomplishment will give you the motivation to continue.

Writing is a tangible way of capturing experiences, struggles, moments of connection, and triumph. If you find that writing is something you genuinely enjoy, you may want to take this practice one step further. Sharing your writing in supportive environments, such as writing groups or workshops, provides a space to connect with others who use writing as a tool for healing. Sharing your work can lead to new perspectives that help you grow into the person you wish to be.

As you explore your emotions through writing, feedback from trusted friends or mentors can be therapeutic. It reinforces the idea that your story is worth telling and that your voice matters.

Writing therapy can be a deeply personal and therapeutic way to explore and process emotions. As you engage with the exercises in this chapter, remember that writing is a tool you can use in whatever way feels right. There's no right or wrong way to write; it's about finding what speaks to you.

Explore Creative Writing

Have you ever had a child ask you to tell them a story? When you start, you don't need to have everything figured out. You just pick a place to start. Exploring writing as a form of therapy is exactly the same. You don't have to have anything figured out. Just start.

Take a look at the list below and pick one or two things to try the next time your emotions are surging.

- Poetry
- Song Lyrics
- Short Story
- Haiku
- Letter of Encouragement
- Free writing
- Journal Entry

CHAPTER 10
ADDRESSING SKEPTICISM AND BARRIERS

"Friends ask you questions; enemies question you."

— CRISS JAMI

It's natural to have questions and doubts about your healing process, especially if you've tried other therapies without success. You might wonder, "How does somatic therapy really work?" or "Is there any science behind it?" You're not alone. Many people are curious about the effectiveness of somatic therapy, so we'll explore some of the science and supportive evidence for anyone who might be skeptical about this path.

Neurobiology is the study of brain and nerve function.

When I started talk therapy, I distinctly remember feeling silly about the things I felt were *traumatic*. I mean, what business did I have in seeking therapy for my childhood abandonment issues when there were *real* horrors going on in the world? And yet, there was one memory that I could not shake from my childhood. It was the day my dad left our home, just before my parents divorced.

It is the earliest and most vivid memory I have of my childhood. I was around six years old, and I am almost completely blocked from all memories before that day. Ironically, I can remember that day like it was yesterday. My mom was hunched over the kitchen counter, crying. My little sister and I were sitting in her playpen in the living room. She was also crying, and I was trying to calm her down. Then, my dad walked past my sister and me and out the front door.

Now, don't get me wrong...I love my dad, and we have a great relationship. My *adult* brain knows that marriage and parenting are two different things. I understand *now* that my feelings of "not being enough" for him to stay had nothing to do with him not loving me...but that day, little me didn't know that. In fact, adolescent me didn't really understand that either, and teenage me was just bitter. They were the versions of me who needed to heal.

Then my therapist pointed out that, for six-year-old me, it **was** the most devastating thing in my life. I didn't have the ability to discern marriage from parenting, or divorce from abandonment. I only knew *I* wasn't enough for him to stay...and my body had not forgotten it. Mind. Blown.

That sweet, little six-year-old version of me could not fathom the repercussions this life event would have on the relationships in my life. I was utterly clueless that my brain would change, *to protect me*, physically and emotionally, *for the rest of my life!* Or, at least until I began seeing my super-amazing therapist.

I was in therapy for many reasons, but primarily, I was tired of bleeding on the people who had not injured me. More specifically, my husband. He had taken the brunt of my emotional damage for years.

That session was a turning point for me, and I decided I no longer wanted to carry the events of my past into my future. We started working on EMDR (Chapter 16), and I have since added more somatic practices to my therapy journey. It's been a game-changer.

All this to say, no matter how small or trivial your trauma *feels* to you today, it is relevant...absolutely and unequivocally relevant... and you deserve to heal.

LET'S GET A LITTLE SCIENCE-Y

The foundation of somatic therapy is in the neurobiology of trauma and its impact on the body. Trauma-related disorders, like PTSD, affect areas of the brain like the amygdala and prefrontal cortex, which regulate your emotions and behavior.

When trauma occurs, it triggers a sequence of changes in the body, influencing hormones, the immune system, and even the gut-brain connection. These changes can present themselves in the body as both psychological and physical symptoms, which creates a need for a type of therapy that addresses the entire body as well.

Somatic therapy does exactly that by focusing on the mind-body connection to promote healing. Recent studies support its effectiveness in trauma recovery, showing positive outcomes in reducing symptoms of PTSD and anxiety. By engaging with physical sensations and promoting body awareness, somatic therapy sparks an emotional release while providing a customizable approach to healing.

Research indicates that body-focused interventions can improve emotional regulation and resilience. For instance, studies have demonstrated that somatic therapy helps reduce PTSD symptoms by promoting a deeper connection between mind and body. These findings are supported by neuroscience, which confirms that somatic practices can alter brain structure and function, creating new neural pathways that lead to profound emotional healing. These studies are just a glimpse into the positive effects of somatic therapy as a viable therapeutic pathway.

Psychologists, trauma specialists, and holistic health practitioners also advocate for somatic therapy and recognize its potential to complement traditional treatments. These professionals understand the importance of engaging the body in the healing process. Their testimonials confirm its effectiveness, reassuring those who may still be wary.

Despite the growing evidence supporting somatic therapy, there are still misconceptions. Some may view it as pseudoscience, or "fake" science, and question its legitimacy. However, it's essential to differentiate somatic therapy from unproven methods.

Somatic therapy is grounded in scientific principles and factual research. It's an evidence-based approach to healing that addresses both the physical and emotional parts of trauma, providing a whole-body approach to recovery. By focusing on present-moment awareness and the body's wisdom, somatic therapy helps individuals access and process their experiences.

Myths & Facts Quiz

Test your understanding of somatic therapy with this quick quiz. Identify whether each statement is a myth or a fact:

1. Somatic therapy is based on scientific principles and research.
2. Somatic therapy is the same as alternative medicine with no scientific backing.
3. Somatic therapy can change brain pathways and improve emotional regulation.
4. Somatic therapy focuses solely on verbal communication to heal trauma.

Answers: 1. Fact; 2. Myth; 3. Fact; 4. Myth

FEAR OF RE-TRAUMATIZATION IN THERAPY

It's completely understandable to worry about re-experiencing trauma during therapy. Many people share this fear, and it's a valid concern that deserves to be addressed. The thought of revisiting painful memories can be debilitating, and you might worry about feeling overwhelmed or vulnerable. But somatic therapy is specifically designed with these fears in mind. It focuses on a trauma-informed approach that prioritizes your safety and comfort throughout the process.

Trauma-informed care ensures that therapy is conducted in a way that respects *your* boundaries and minimizes the risk of distress. This means your therapist is trained to create a supportive environment where you feel safe and secure. Your therapist will prioritize your comfort and safety by carefully pacing sessions and using techniques that gently guide you through the healing process.

Somatic therapy uses a range of techniques to reduce the risk of re-traumatization. One of these techniques is gradual exposure and titration of trauma memories. This approach involves gradually introducing and processing traumatic memories in small, manageable amounts. By doing so, you remain in control and are less likely to become overwhelmed.

Grounding techniques are especially helpful during these times, keeping you present while maintaining a sense of control during therapy. You may be asked to focus on your breath and notice the physical sensations in your body, or you may use sensory objects like a stress ball. These techniques anchor you in the present, preventing you from being swept away by recalling past experiences. This connection and presence reduce the chance of re-traumatization.

Communicating your fears with your therapist is an important step in building a supportive relationship. It's okay to express your concerns and discuss any fears. A good therapist will welcome this dialogue and work with you to develop a personal treatment plan. This plan should consider your needs and comfort levels, incorporating strategies that help you feel safe.

Establishing clear boundaries is also essential. You might want to agree on safe words or signals to help you communicate if you feel uncomfortable or need to pause. This level of collaboration ensures that therapy proceeds at a pace that feels right for you.

MAKING TIME FOR SOMATIC PRACTICES IN BUSY LIVES

While participating in a women's weight loss group, I distinctly remember hearing another member voice her frustration. She was eating right, exercising, and drinking more water, but the scale was going in the wrong direction, and had been for several weeks. She was at her breaking point and on the verge of quitting the program. She bravely shared her feelings with the group.

> *"My life feels like a never-ending juggling act. Between work, family responsibilities, hormone changes, and the constant demands of life, finding time for healthy eating and exercise feels impossible. The thought of adding something else, like self-care, makes me feel physically ill. I just can't stretch myself any farther."*

Sound familiar? For most women, the pressure of being *everything* for *everyone* is often the scale that measures our success. In most cases, the easiest thing to sacrifice is self-care. It's so easy to put your needs on the back burner, telling yourself that you'll focus on yourself once things slow down. But let's be honest, life rarely slows down. Instead, it speeds up, leaving you feeling like you're always playing catch-up.

Balancing work, family, and self-care is a challenge many of us face, and the guilt of prioritizing personal wellness doesn't help. You might think, "How can I take time for myself when there's so much to do?" This mindset is common; It's how most of us were raised. But we're older now. Wiser. And, it's time to look in the mirror and remind the person staring back that investing in herself isn't selfish. It's necessary. Invest in her like you would invest in your daughter, your sister, or your dearest friend.

BUILD YOUR PRACTICE SCHEDULE

Creating a practice schedule is a big step in your somatic journey. When you build your schedule, consider your commitment to healing, and schedule your practices like any other appointments, meetings, or doctor's visits.

Set achievable goals, starting small and gradually increasing your practice time as you become more comfortable. Don't focus on how much time you have to give, just give what you can…consistently. Establishing a routine that works with your existing commitments makes it easier to stick with your practices and make them a natural part of your day.

You'll begin to notice an improvement in your quality of life. Stress levels may decrease, and your sense of healthfulness might increase. Perhaps the best of all is the satisfaction that comes from feeling more balanced and in control, which can make a huge impact on both your mental and physical health.

Some days, life will throw you a lot of roadblocks. Try to honor your commitments to yourself in the best way you can. As you continue on this path, you'll find that the time you invest in yourself is never wasted time.

CHAPTER 11
CASE STUDIES AND SUCCESS STORIES

"Trauma is a fact of life. It does not, however, have to be a life sentence."

— PETER A. LEVINE

P icture yourself at the edge of an ocean, with waves carrying stories of resilience, healing, and transformation. Much like the ocean, the stories you are about to read will reveal the depth and scale of somatic healing. They are the lived experiences of individuals who have been on their paths to healing, often finding peace and strength in places they never thought possible. This chapter is a collection of those real-life transformations.

These shared stories tell the power of somatic therapy when addressing trauma, chronic pain, PTSD, and more. Each narrative is evidence that healing lies within us all, waiting to be discovered and nurtured.

STACIE | *PTSD*

I had a forced abortion at 19. I came from a divorced family. My husband and I had a son, and we were having some marital struggles. He did not want another baby, and I was scared of losing the family we had built.

I remember being so scared, sad, and heartbroken as I walked in for the procedure, but so fragile and empty when it was done. I was given a sedative to relax me for the procedure, but I was in and out of consciousness. I think I was fighting it in a way.

I heard the doctor say, "Probably would have been a beautiful little girl." Then I heard what sounded like a metal trash can lid opening and closing. In my mind, they threw my baby away like trash. I felt worthless and unworthy of a happy life.

I still have flashbacks when I see metal trash cans with the foot pedal, and I get anxiety when anything medical arises in my life or the lives of those I love.

I wish I could hold that version of myself and tell her, 'Don't do it.' I want her to understand that she doesn't have to allow anyone to force her to do something. I am still working on forgiving myself.

I find comfort in my grandchildren and watching them grow. I always do what I can to help others because I felt so alone at that time in my life. I want to fix others, because nobody was able to fix me.

Art therapy has been an important part of my somatic experience. It helps to relax me and calm my emotions during times of anxiety. I am working on incorporating positive affirmations to continue my healing process and breathing techniques to control my anxiety and chronic pain.

WENDY | *Childhood Trauma*

I am not sure what started it or how long it lasted. As an eight-year-old, what seemed like minutes when I was younger was more than likely hours. It was dark out, and I was thirsty; my parents were in the hall bathroom. We heard the screaming and things falling, but I didn't register it as fighting.

My dad opened the door, and I asked for a drink. He pushed my mom out of the bathroom. She fell to the floor, and he pushed her all the way to the kitchen, where he made her give me a drink. She gave me a ginger ale. I do not like ginger ale, and I remember complaining. He jerked the bottle from me and started hitting my mom with the bottle while screaming at her because she didn't know that I didn't like it. When he noticed we were watching, he made her go back into the bathroom.

At some point, the screams became scary, and then dead silence. I banged on the door, waiting for an answer, while trying repeatedly to open the door. I then grabbed my siblings, and we climbed out the window. We started knocking on several of the neighbors' doors until someone opened the door, and I asked them to call the police.

We waited outside for the police. When they came, they took my dad; my mom refused treatment. Once everyone was gone, we went to check on my mom. She wouldn't leave the bathroom. It was a scene from a horror film. The door frame, sink, vanity, and closet were all broken and covered in blood. I remember red. So much red. The smell of rusty nails is still triggering to me because I'm reminded of the smell of blood. There were also several holes in the wall.

We went to be with my mom, and she suddenly became enraged. She started yelling at us. She was screaming over and over for us to clean the bathroom as if it were our fault. I remember being so tired. I did not understand, and I felt completely alone.

That night changed how I viewed my life. The two people who were supposed to protect me, no matter what, did just the opposite. I lost all faith and trust in people. It made me asocial, and I overly analyze everything. As I got older, I became very independent. I also made a promise that my kids would never feel alone.

To this day, my adult son knows that there will never be a time when I will not be there for him. I still don't like it when anger is directed at me. I often shut down, walk away, and find a dark, cold place to reset. I will sit and listen to really loud music until it passes.

I wish I could make people understand that there are reasons I am quick to push people away. There are reasons I am full of doubt and automatically think the worst.

Art therapy has helped me heal over time. I love crafting, and I feel so at peace when I am invested in a project. I find comfort in the rain or a quiet walk. Especially walking on the beach or in a park. I can simply be present without heavy thoughts or worries. It's my form of meditation. Reading is also a great escape. I love getting lost in a good book.

Ultimately, I know that my parents' volatile relationship wasn't my fault. It wasn't my siblings' fault either. Our parents were just unhappy and in a situation neither wanted to be in. I know they could not leave because they had children, but I wish I could tell that to 8-year-old me and my siblings. They were never at fault. I was never at fault. I wish I could hold them all and tell them that we will be okay. I want to tell them that I'll never abandon them, and I'll always be there if they need me.

STEPHANIE | *Unexpected Death of A Loved One*

I lost JP (my high school sweetheart) to suicide. He was the love of my life, my best friend. My everything. But we had different dreams for our futures, so we had broken up.

I loved him deeply, so I dissociated myself from everything and everyone. I quit my job, moved away, and started spiraling. Eventually, I reconnected with an old boyfriend, and we were engaged about a year later. I was newly engaged when I found out that JP attempted to take his own life. He lived for five weeks after he pulled the trigger.

Trauma really changes the way you think of yourself and the compromises you make for comfort. Those five weeks JP was in the hospital, I became a different person. I told so many lies to cover up the time I spent at his bedside. Lies to work. Lies to my fiancé. Lies to my family. Lies to myself. Guilt that still has a hold on me, every single day.

For the longest time, I told myself that I was not a good enough friend, companion, or person if I couldn't support someone enough to do something as basic as breathe. It wasn't true, of course, but it was a belief I felt in my core, and it was shaped by experiencing such a traumatic event. I still struggle with sadness and have constant thoughts of what I could have done to change the outcome.

I wish I could sit myself down, look her in the eyes, hold her hand, and let her know that it's not her responsibility to make sure someone stays alive. She can't control it, and it's not her fault. Funerals are hard. I have trouble listening to certain songs, and I feel sick when I witness someone being intoxicated or having suicidal thoughts, even in a movie. July 28th is always a rough day. Sometimes his laugh plays over and over in my head, and I always get a little sad when I see his initials somewhere.

I've learned to compartmentalize...to an extreme. Sometimes, I push it so far down that it feels like it happened to someone else. But, I died too all those years ago, and in return, someone else had to rise in my place. So, I grieve not only him but the old me as well...every day, after almost 28 years. I have created a shell to keep myself guarded from anything that may hurt.

I have a horrible fear of abandonment. I'm constantly scared that people will leave me when I least expect it. My therapist and I are working on my coping mechanisms. When the memories are too much to bear, I talk to him and believe he hears me. It's like the movie Ghost when they are still here, but we don't see them, and sometimes we get to connect. I had never given any real thought to healing because I always felt that healing meant accepting what happened and letting go. So, I've held onto my trauma because I don't want to forget him. But, I am learning that healing doesn't have to mean forgetting.

I can truly empathize with anyone dealing with sudden loss. You will eventually be able to breathe, but grief is forever. It's definitely a process, but I'm trying to turn those traumatic memories into positive ones so I can honor him in a way that feels good. I think I need to work on trust as well. Trust that things will work out so I don't have to live in such a state of fear.

I don't have it all figured out yet, but I owe it to myself to try. I think he would want that for me. And, I want it for me too.

JOLIE | *Childhood Trauma*

The first time I saw my mother using, we were in a Popeyes bathroom. I was about 6 or 7 years old. I still remember the orange painted walls. She told me to stand in the corner and turn around. Being a child, of course, I peeked and I saw her with a needle in her arm. I remember having a pit in my stomach because even though I didn't exactly understand what she was doing, I knew it was very wrong.

I think her using stripped me of my childhood, and I quickly realized that I had to lock into being alert at all times. To this day, I always notice the signs of someone being high, and I'm very uneasy when around those who are high. I've also had extreme anxiety since I was a child, that I still experience.

Today, I am able to remind myself that I am no longer a helpless child in a horrible situation. I am an adult with the ability to remove myself from situations that make me uncomfortable or potentially dangerous. If I could go back and talk to 6-year-old me, I would tell her that she didn't deserve to be exposed to that situation, and it is not her job to fix her parent.

I still live with the effects of those events. It plays a huge part in me feeling like my life has to go a certain way, or I failed. It motivates me to be a good mom and to raise my son in a way that he will never ever feel the emotions or be put through the things that I had to go through. I chose not to follow the same footsteps. Instead of letting it be an excuse for falling into the cycle, I used it as motivation to be better.

I have an extremely supportive family that understands mental health. I now have a relationship with my mother, and I speak to her about the events that happened, explaining to her how they made me feel. She doesn't remember many of the details, but I remember everything. It's very helpful to get some validation for the things that I went through. That feels good.

I'm working on finding the courage to speak up about things that I dislike. I've always had a fear of people being mad at me, so I feel like a lot of the things I do are to appease others, so that I'm not hurting anyone. I am learning to set boundaries and express myself without fear of upsetting others. It feels amazing!

The growth that each of these women has achieved is a testament to the positive impact of somatic healing. Their self-awareness has evolved to better recognize and respond to their emotional and physical needs.

Relationships have improved, communication has become more authentic, and the quality of their lives has changed. But the thing that makes me so hopeful is that their stories are just beginning, and will continue to improve as each of these brave women embraces their somatic journey.

Healing is possible for you. For me. For anyone…regardless of their background or their trauma.

> **Reflection Section**
>
> Take a moment to reflect on these stories. Did you notice any similarities to your experiences? Did any aspects stand out to you? Try recalling a time when you felt a strong connection with your body or emotions. What did you learn from that moment? How might somatic therapy support your healing journey?

DIVERSE JOURNEYS: SOMATIC THERAPY ACROSS CULTURES

Somatic therapy draws from the wisdom of many cultures, each contributing unique approaches to healing. In many parts of the world, traditional healing practices have long embraced the connection between mind and body. This is a principle that is at the core of somatic therapy.

Indigenous cultures often incorporate rituals that engage the senses and spirit. This approach helps to ground individuals in the present and helps them reconnect with their bodies.

These practices blend somatic therapy with a holistic approach that honors both the physical and spiritual worlds. The cultural perception of body awareness varies, but the core idea remains universal: true healing arises when we listen to our bodies and embrace their wisdom.

---------------- ----------------

SOFIA | *Integrating Cultural Aspects*

Growing up, Sofia always felt a disconnect between the modern world's demands and her cultural roots. Dance therapy helped her bridge that gap. "The rhythm of the drum and the communal dances became more than a way to express my culture. When I danced, it felt like therapy. The rhythm of the drum beat helped to ground me in the moment."

Blending cultural traditions with somatic practices can complement each other in the healing process, providing support that modern methods alone might not achieve.

Cross-cultural somatic therapy isn't without its challenges. Language and communication barriers can hinder the therapeutic process, especially when working with individuals from diverse backgrounds. A good therapist will be attuned to these nuances, bringing patience and empathy to ensure you feel heard and understood.

Cultural beliefs and practices also play a big role in how therapy is perceived and received. Some cultures may view body awareness and expression differently, requiring therapists to adapt their methods with greater respect and sensitivity. This adaptability ensures that therapy remains relevant and respectful, honoring the diverse identities and experiences of each individual.

What I love about these stories is that, despite our differences, the shared experience of trauma and the desire for healing transcends any cultural boundaries.

Across the globe, people have found relief and affirmation through somatic practices. Testimonials from practitioners speak to its widespread impact, reiterating how somatic therapy connects with people from all walks of life.

From densely populated cities to remote indigenous communities, somatic therapy provides a common language that speaks healing, support, and strength to the heart and body.

CHAPTER 12
ENHANCING THE MIND-BODY CONNECTION

"The body keeps the score."

— BESSEL VAN DER KOLK

Have you ever noticed how your mood can affect your body? Perhaps a stressful day leaves your shoulders tense, or a joyful moment brings a pep to your step. This connection between your thoughts, emotions, and physical state is an example of the mind-body connection.

Although the mind-body connection concept has existed for centuries, modern science has only just started to understand its full impact. Your body and mind are like professional dance partners, each guiding the other's moves. When one is out of sync, they both begin to struggle, but when they move together in harmony, the result is beautiful to witness.

Metaphors aside, the mind-body connection is fundamental to restorative health. Think of your nervous system as a bridge, linking your thoughts and emotions to your body's responses. It's like a complex highway system where signals travel back and forth, influencing everything from your heart rate to your digestion.

When you get stressed, your nervous system sends signals that can increase your heart rate and elevate stress hormones. But when you're relaxed, it promotes healing and balance. Traditional Chinese and Indian Ayurvedic medicine have long recognized this connection, stressing the importance of maintaining balance between mind and body for optimal health.

Ancient cultures often viewed the body and mind as inseparable, and diseases were seen as imbalances in this relationship. In ancient Greece, Hippocrates believed that health was achieved by balancing the four humors, which encompassed both the physical and emotional self. Similarly, traditional Chinese medicine links the mental and physical states in the flow of "qi," or life energy, which is essential for health and wellness.

More recently, researchers have begun to validate these ancient beliefs, and some studies using brain imaging have shown that areas of the brain responsible for movement are closely connected with the areas that regulate emotions and consciousness.

Chronic stress can weaken your immune system, making you more susceptible to things like heart disease or diabetes. On the other hand, emotional well-being can promote physical recovery, helping your body heal faster and more effectively.

By learning your body's signals, you can identify stress-induced symptoms early and address them before they become serious.

Techniques like mindfulness and meditation keep you emotionally balanced and can teach you to hear your body's whispers before they become screams.

> ### Mind-Body Awareness Exercise
> Take a moment to sit quietly and focus on your body. Notice any areas of tension or discomfort. As you breathe deeply, envision your breath flowing into these areas, bringing relaxation and release. Did any emotions or thoughts arise during this exercise?

PHYSICAL MANIFESTATIONS OF EMOTIONAL STATES

You might be familiar with the feeling of a pounding headache after a stressful day, or the churning stomach that seems to accompany anxiety like an uninvited guest. These are prime examples of how emotions can manifest physically in the body.

Stress is often a culprit, leading to headaches or migraines. The tension in your mind might decide to camp out in your temples, creating a throbbing reminder of the stress you've been carrying.

Similarly, anxiety doesn't just stay in your mind; it often takes a detour through your digestive system. You might experience nausea, an upset stomach, or even more chronic issues like irritable bowel syndrome. These digestive troubles remind us that anxiety isn't just an emotion, but a full-body experience.

Perhaps, on occasion, you've experienced the muscle tension that creeps in when anger or frustration floods your body. Your shoulders start to rise toward your ears, your jaw begins to clench, and it feels as if your body is bracing for a storm. Each physical symptom is a signal from your body that something needs attention.

Chronic stress can lead to serious long-term health concerns. When stress becomes your constant companion, it can strain your cardiovascular system, leading to hypertension (high blood pressure) and increasing your risk of heart disease. Over time, this continuous pressure can wear down your body, leaving you vulnerable to chronic illness.

Chronic stress is also linked to inflammation in the body, which can contribute to many conditions, including chronic pain syndrome. This kind of pain doesn't just come and go; it lingers, becoming a part of daily life and affecting your quality of life.

Somatization is a term that might sound very technical, but it's something many people experience without realizing it. It refers to the process where emotional distress becomes physical symptoms, even when there is no clear medical cause.

Have you ever felt inexplicably tired, even after a good night's sleep? Or perhaps you've dealt with skin issues that flare up during times of emotional turmoil? These are examples of somatization.

Unexplained fatigue and lethargy can be your body's way of expressing emotional exhaustion. Similarly, skin conditions like eczema or psoriasis can worsen when you become stressed or anxious. Yes. That's right. Emotional distress can quite literally get under your skin.

Understanding somatization helps you see these symptoms as meaningful messages from your body, instead of passing them off as random ailments.

What is somatization?

Somatization is the conversion of a mental state (such as depression or anxiety) into physical symptoms. Merriam-Webster also defines somatization as the existence of physical bodily complaints in the absence of a known medical condition.

For persistent symptoms that don't improve, seek professional guidance. A healthcare provider or therapist can work with you to tailor strategies that address both the emotional and physical aspects of your care.

HARNESSING THE MIND-BODY LINK FOR HEALING

When was the last time you got lost in a daydream? You zone out. Your body becomes relaxed, and your breathing slows. You might not even realize it happened until something snaps you out of it. (Hands up if it's ever happened at work, and something startles you back to reality as you search frantically around the room to see if you've been caught. Yeah, me too.)

But, what if you could do that on purpose, and use it as a tool for healing? That is the exact purpose of visualization and imagery exercises.

Visualization and imagery can transform how you manage pain and stress. By picturing yourself in a peaceful setting, you can shift your mental state, calming your nervous system and reducing physical discomfort. This technique nudges your body to follow your mind's lead, easing tension and promoting relaxation.

Standing Among Giants | 2018 - Muir Woods National Monument, CA

As I shared with you in Chapter 2, Muir Woods is that place for me. There is a grounding type of connection that I feel when I visit a forest full of larger-than-life trees. It is humbling for me to stand among these pillars of strength as they surround me in a protective hug that only Mother Nature herself could offer.

When stress, anxiety, or negative thoughts weigh heavily on me, I retreat to Muir Woods in my mind. I feel the gentle breeze moving between the trees. I smell the richness of the earth's soil that has helped to root these gentle giants for hundreds of years. I see the sun's rays shining through the branches, casting various shapes on the forest floor. I feel and hear the crunch of the leaves beneath my feet as I walk the footpaths of those who have explored before me. I take in deep, grateful breaths of the oxygen the forest provides. And, if I allow myself to be fully immersed in this mental escape, I can feel myself entering a state of blissful calm. My heart rate slows. My breathing becomes deep and intentional. My body relaxes as it releases the unwanted tension. And, while I wish with everything in me that I could be there physically, I don't have to leave the room to be transported to my safe space.

For some who suffer with chronic pain, visualizing the pain as a color or a shape that gradually fades can sometimes diminish its grip, and gently guide their minds toward a state of calm.

Remember those positive affirmations we discussed in Chapter 7? When you tell yourself, "I am strong and resilient," or "My body is healing each day," you're not just saying empty words. You're planting seeds of belief that can influence your physical health.

Studies suggest that positive affirmations can lead to actual changes in the body's stress response, helping to lower blood pressure and reduce anxiety. Regularly practicing your affirmations supports a healing mindset and gives you a sense of control over your health.

There are many other fascinating technologies that focus on your body's inner workings. These techniques involve monitoring physical signals like heart rate and brainwave patterns, providing real-time feedback. During biofeedback sessions, patients wear a device that shows their heart rate variability on a screen. With this visual feedback, they learn to regulate breathing and relax their muscles, improving the heart's response to stress.

Neurofeedback goes a step further by focusing on the brain's activity and training your brainwave patterns through exercises that promote relaxation. Neurofeedback can improve mental clarity and emotional stability, turning the mind-body connection into a skill you can develop to combat stress. So cool!

Last, but not least, we will circle back to integrating movement with mindfulness. We talked about yoga and tai chi earlier. They are perfect examples of practices that focus on breath and movement. Both help to restore balance and calm the mind. When you flow through a series of yoga poses, and each movement is synchronized with your breath, you focus on being present in your body.

Did you know?

Yoga is wonderful for stretching and strengthening muscles. It also centers the mind, creating a harmonious experience.

With its deliberate, graceful movements, Tai Chi promotes mental clarity and physical balance.

CHAPTER 13
NAVIGATING CHRONIC CONDITIONS

"Unexpressed emotions tend to stay in the body like small ticking time bombs—they are illnesses in incubation."

— MARILYN VAN M. DERBUR

How would you navigate a life where every step and movement is followed by a persistent ache? For those living with chronic pain, this is a daily reality. Not only are they dealing with the physical discomfort of their condition, but they also experience the emotional toll. This 1-2 punch can often create a cycle of pain and stress that's hard to break.

Visually, I relate chronic pain to a spider web that, over time, extends into all areas of your life. A small trigger can set off a delicate web of events, linking physical pain to stress, fatigue, and other emotions in a way that's hard to separate or control.

Where acute pain serves as a warning signal for immediate harm, chronic pain lingers long after the initial injury has healed, and sometimes without a clear cause. It's as if the body has developed a habit of hurting, influenced by additional factors like anxiety and depression. Coming to terms with the physical changes in your body can be difficult emotionally and mentally. This is where somatic therapy steps in to untangle the web of pain and emotions that hold you captive.

Chronic pain can suck the life right out of you. The physical pain can be debilitating. But for many, the physical aspect is just the tip of the iceberg. Chronic pain is exhausting. Mentally and physically exhausting.

In all honesty, before being diagnosed with autoimmune disease, it never occurred to me that other people didn't have pain all the time. Like, no joke. Initially, I thought I was just getting older. I mean, I was approaching 50, so I thought it was normal to start feeling different in my body. But the effects extended so much farther than my physical pain.

I suffered loss of stamina, low tolerance, agitation, loss of mobility, and depression. I was in therapy. I was doing the work. Surely this was just to be expected with aging, right? One day, my therapist asked me how I was doing "coming to terms" with my life now that chronic illness and chronic pain had entered the equation.

The question hit me like a ton of bricks. I hadn't even considered it, really. I was still in a state of survival, and to be honest, I was simply taking things day by day. My brain couldn't think that far ahead. At that point, I was just trying to make it through the work day.

I didn't realize that coming to terms with the "chronic" aspects of my life meant starting to worry that my dreams might not come to fruition. Plans might need to change. Goals might have to pivot. My body might need me to adjust...to accommodate.

Ew.

No one wants to hear that. It's like finally, after years of struggling financially, you're able to get your dream car. Then, when you take it home, you start to realize that your body is struggling to get in and out of the driver's seat. It's debilitating, and sad, and it can send you into an endless spiral.

Let's dig a little deeper to better understand the pain cycle. Chronic pain often starts with a trigger, perhaps an injury or an underlying health condition. Over time, this pain can become a constant presence, even when the original cause is no longer apparent.

Emotional stressors, like grief or trauma, can exacerbate this cycle, creating a feedback loop where stress heightens pain, and pain increases stress. What. The. Actual. Heck! (Yes, I'm keeping it PG here.) This cycle can feel relentless, leaving you feeling trapped in your own body.

Somatic therapy works with you to break this cycle by focusing on the body's sensations and responses, helping you gain control over your pain.

USING YOUR BREATH

When managing chronic pain, breathwork becomes an essential tool. I know what you are thinking...does everything come back to breathwork? Well, no...and yes. You see, controlled breathing techniques can change how our bodies perceive pain signals, and mastering these techniques can greatly reduce the stress associated with chronic pain. Oh, so *now* I have your attention.

Diaphragmatic breathing, or belly breathing, is particularly effective for chronic pain. By focusing on deep, slow breaths, you can activate the body's relaxation response, lowering pain intensity and promoting calm. Integrating breath awareness into daily activities, like during a walk or when sitting quietly, can help maintain a sense of control and ease throughout your day.

CREATE A PAIN MANAGEMENT PLAN

If you're managing chronic pain, you need a pain management plan. It's not a question, really. It's not even a suggestion. I'm telling you that you *need* to figure that out. So, let's kick it off.

Start by identifying your personal pain triggers and responses. This might include certain activities, stressors, or even specific times of day when pain flares up. Once you understand these triggers, you can set realistic goals for pain reduction and mobility improvement, tailoring somatic practices to your unique needs.

Maybe you want to practice progressive muscle relaxation daily or integrate gentle movement exercises into your morning routine. Whatever your goals, remember that progress is personal and incremental. **Celebrate small victories.** A day with less pain, or a moment of relaxation, is a positive stop along your healing path.

My Pain Management Checklist

- Identify and list common pain triggers.
- Choose three somatic techniques to try this week.
- Set a realistic goal: e.g., practice breathing exercises for 10 minutes daily.
- Reflect on your progress at the end of the week. What feels like it's working? Where would you like to improve next week?

COPING WITH CHRONIC ILLNESS: MINDFUL LIVING

Living with a chronic illness is like navigating a path that constantly shifts beneath your feet. The physical challenges are often met with emotional and social hurdles, each demanding your attention and resilience.

Fatigue becomes a familiar companion, stealing your energy at the most inconvenient times. Some days, even getting out of bed can feel like an insurmountable task. Working through these fluctuations requires more than physical stamina; it demands a mental grit that can be exhausting to maintain.

The psychological weight of chronic illness is heavy, often leading to feelings of frustration, isolation, or even depression. It's a burden that extends beyond the individual. You might notice it affecting your relationships and social interactions, as loved ones may struggle to understand the invisible battles you face daily.

You need something more than a cookie-cutter plan. You need a path forward that addresses the physical symptoms you endure, and the emotional and social aspects of living with a chronic condition.

> **"By practicing mindful acceptance, you learn to live alongside your physical limitations rather than constantly battling them."**

Mindfulness can be a source of inspiration on this complex path, teaching you to cope with your pain while living more fully. Yes, challenges may arise, but your mindfulness practice will help you accept the present moment, even if that moment is filled with discomfort or pain. This acceptance is about finding peace with your reality.

You aren't raising the white flag, so don't see it as defeat. By practicing mindful acceptance, you learn to live alongside your physical limitations rather than constantly battling them. It also encourages you to shift your focus from illness to wellness, a powerful change in how you perceive your path.

Practicing gratitude can be beneficial in this regard. Even on the toughest days, finding small things to be thankful for can help reframe your experiences.

Adding mindfulness to your daily routine doesn't require big gestures or unreasonable time investments. Simple practices can bring you a sense of presence and calm.

Mindful eating is one such practice. It's about savoring each bite and appreciating all of the flavors and textures of your food. This turns meals from hurried necessities into moments of mindfulness and gratitude. It is also great for your digestion!

Walking meditation is another gentle way to incorporate mindfulness. As you walk, pay attention to the sensations of your feet touching the ground and the rhythm of your breath. Notice the fluid motion of putting one foot in front of the other. This shift in your focus grounds you in the present while providing physical activity. It's a form of "moving meditation" that calms the mind.

The gifts of mindful living go beyond the immediate relief of stress. For those with chronic illnesses, mindfulness is essential for emotional regulation. It provides a toolkit for reducing stress, conditioning you to respond to situations thoughtfully rather than reactively. This can also help to improve sleep quality, as a calmer mind makes it easier to drift into restful slumber.

Wellness is not the absence of illness. Wellness is the ability to focus on the positive to create a rich, fulfilling life, even **with** the presence of chronic conditions. Mindfulness doesn't promise to erase the challenges, but it shows us how to live among them peacefully, finding moments of joy and contentment amidst the struggles.

ENHANCING QUALITY OF LIFE WITH SOMATIC PRACTICES

When you're living with a chronic condition, the concept of quality of life becomes a focal point. We want to manage symptoms, but we also need to find joy and fulfillment each day.

The goal of somatic therapy is to encourage a shift in perspective, changing limitations to abilities. It's a conscious decision to focus on what you can do rather than what you can't. I know...I know. Easier said than done. Below are a few ways to shift that perspective and reclaim control of our lives.

MOVEMENT - Regular gentle movement is one way somatic therapy supports physical vitality. In the last chapter, we touched on some of the benefits of yoga and tai chi for combining movement with mindfulness. These body-based practices can rejuvenate your spirit while keeping you active and engaged.

These exercises also help to keep you flexible and strong, which makes daily activities more manageable and enjoyable. By being present in your body, you communicate more effectively, responding with empathy and understanding.

CREATIVE EXPRESSION - Creative expression is another outlet for emotional release, giving you a safe space to explore your feelings and experiences. Whether through art, music, or dance, these activities provide time to express what words cannot, offering a multitude of ways to experience relief and gain perspective.

These types of expression tap into a part of you that is intuitive and healing, where emotions flow freely and transform into something tangible and beautiful. The creative process can be incredibly therapeutic, helping you process trauma in a way that feels authentic and freeing.

LYSA | *Gentle Yoga*

My doctor's office posted a flyer for a Gentle Yoga class. I have Fibromyalgia and haven't had success with any exercise program. It's hard to move when everything hurts, and when you move too much, everything hurts more. I was always tired, but I decided to go because I really wanted to stay active. I always thought exercise had to be intense cardio and strength training, but there was something so powerful about the slow, gentle movements and the focus on my breath. I got a great workout and left feeling relaxed and at peace. I always thought movement had to equal pain, but yoga taught me otherwise.

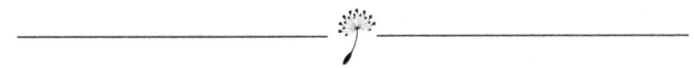

SUPPORT NETWORKS - Community and support networks are there to build connections with others who understand your experiences. Whether in person or online, these groups provide a safe space to share stories, exchange advice, and give encouragement, creating a sense of belonging and shared understanding.

Joining support groups or therapy collectives can spark empathy and compassion as you learn and grow alongside others on similar pathways. These communities give much more than support. The solidarity and connection that some experience can be deeply nourishing.

KAT | *Group Support*

I isolated myself for a long time. I was sick, and my mental health was the worst it's ever been. I constantly felt like a burden to others, so I simply removed myself from the outside world. And, I spiraled…for a while. I dissociated for a long time. After finding an awesome therapist and doing some intense work, we started talking about ways to reconnect with my family and friends. But I felt so out of touch, and I dreaded the thought of answering endless questions about my health. She told me about a local group that had therapy sessions at the community center.

It took everything in me to walk through the door for that first session. I sat ALL the way in the back, like the last chair in the corner. It's funny to me now, but I was so scared then. I was practically hiding under the hood of my sweatshirt. The second time I went, the chairs were set up in a circle. I almost ran back to my car. No hiding this time. But everyone was so nice and welcoming. After hearing others' stories and eventually sharing mine, I found the courage to fix my relationships. My mom and I are on the right path now. I've still got some work to do, but it's nice to know we are on good terms. I lost some friends after my depression, but I've accepted it. It just showed me who was really in my corner. And, I made some really supportive new friends who won't judge me if things get tough again.

CHAPTER 14

BUILDING COMMUNITY AND SUPPORT

"The wound is the place where the light enters you."

— RUMI

For some, the idea of joining a support group is a hard pass. The vulnerability and retelling of negative memories, along with the emotions that resurface, is further validation to stay as far away as possible. For others, making contact with individuals who can identify with their hardships, relate to their worries, and encourage them to keep going, is a no-brainer. Usually, these two unique personalities marry each other. I'm kidding...but only about the last part.

Humor me for a minute. In Chapter 12, I told you about my love of nature. In particular, I walked you through my visualization of Muir Wood. So, let's use that example to talk about community and networking as we think about the strength of the individual tree when compared to the forest.

A single tree stands alone, exposed to strong winds and harsh conditions while relying solely on the strength of its own roots to stay upright. In a forest, each tree grows beside many others, and their roots become strongly connected and nourish the soil.

Their shared support and resources are a quiet network of strength. At the same time, they protect and shelter the saplings and weaker trees that grow beneath them.

In the same way, support groups bring similar people together. Each person strengthens the group through personal connection, understanding, and support. Growing together while sheltering those on weaker ground. Alone, healing is hard. Together, like the forest, we can thrive, heal, and withstand what once felt impossible.

When you engage with others who share your commitment to somatic healing, you find emotional reinforcement that validates your experiences. This validation is powerful; it reminds you that you're not alone and that others understand and share your desire to change.

Having a support network also means you have people to encourage you to maintain your somatic practices. They will celebrate your small victories and gently nudge you when you need a reminder to return to your planned practices. This encouragement can be the difference between staying on track and feeling disconnected.

Your network has the ability to create a dynamic learning environment where everyone grows from shared knowledge and experiences. Initially, you might receive many new techniques or perspectives from your fellow group members. However, over time, you may discover that you are both the recipient and giver, tapping into your shared knowledge and experiences to empathize deeply with others.

The thought of group therapy might seem daunting at first, but there are several paths you can explore. Local therapy or wellness groups often host gatherings focused on somatic healing. These groups can be a great starting point to connect with others who share similar goals.

Community centers frequently host workshops or classes dedicated to somatic practices, providing educational opportunities and a chance to meet like-minded individuals. These local opportunities for face-to-face connections can nurture your sense of community and belonging.

Once you've identified potential networks, building and nurturing these relationships takes intention and effort. Attend regular meetings or events to show your commitment and become a familiar face within the group. Consistency builds trust, making it easier to create meaningful bonds.

Don't be afraid to initiate one-on-one connections as well. Sometimes, deeper relationships form when you take the time to have individual conversations over coffee or during a walk. These seemingly insignificant interactions can become an integral part of your growth.

Aim for diversity within your network. Engaging with people from various backgrounds and experiences broadens your understanding of the world around you, often revealing an entirely new perspective. Multicultural groups can bring together multiple practices and viewpoints. This diversity can introduce you to alternative approaches, encourage flexibility, and help you tailor your healing to fit your unique needs. By opening yourself to other cultures and perspectives, you'll tap into your sense of empathy and personal growth.

This checklist can help you find and cultivate a support network that nurtures your somatic process with richness and diversity.

Support Network Exploration

- Identify Local Resources: List local therapy groups, wellness centers, or community classes that focus on somatic healing.
- Attend an Event: Choose one group or class to attend this month and jot down your impressions.
- Initiate a Conversation: Reach out to someone from the event for a one-on-one chat to build a deeper connection.
- Diversity: Consider the diversity within your network. Are there perspectives or cultures you'd like to explore further?
- Set a Goal: Define a personal goal for your support network, such as establishing a new connection or sharing a difficult story by the end of the season.

ONLINE COMMUNITIES: SHARING AND LEARNING TOGETHER

Despite the fixation with the latest TikTok trends, the internet can be a lifeline for those who are homebound, introverted, or living in remote areas. The prospect of an online community gives access to a unique space where you can connect, share, and support others, regardless of physical or geographical boundaries.

Online communities bring together people from different backgrounds and experiences, diversifying the healing process. The anonymity these spaces provide can also be a powerful draw. Many people feel safer sharing personal stories and exploring sensitive topics behind the protection of their computer screen. This privacy can encourage more open and honest exchanges, allowing individuals to express themselves without fear of judgment or stigma.

Several online platforms have emerged as resources for those seeking somatic support. Facebook groups dedicated to somatic therapy are vibrant communities where members post questions, share experiences, and ask for advice. These groups often have moderators who guide discussions and ensure the space remains supportive and focused.

Similarly, Reddit hosts a somatic therapy subreddit, which provides a forum for individuals to engage and discuss various somatic practices.

These platforms create a sense of belonging, where members can find comfort in the shared understanding of others on their personal healing journey.

Dedicated apps for mindfulness and community support, like Insight Timer or Calm, also provide spaces for connection. These apps often include groups where users can interact, discuss challenges, and celebrate successes together.

While online communities appeal to many, they also come with challenges. One major advantage is the instant access to diverse perspectives. Engaging with individuals from different backgrounds and experiences can broaden your understanding and introduce you to new approaches to somatic healing. However, the vast amount of information available can sometimes be overwhelming.

Misinformation or unverified advice can circulate, potentially leading to confusion or missteps in your healing process. Approach online interactions with a critical eye. Verify information through reputable sources and consult a trained professional when in doubt.

To make the most of online communities, consider a couple of guidelines for engaging effectively and safely.

- Set clear boundaries for your online interactions. Determine what you're comfortable sharing and what you'd prefer to keep private. This boundary-setting helps to protect yourself emotionally and ensures that your online experience remains positive.
- Actively share your experiences and resources with the community. By contributing aspects of your story, you support the group relationship in which all members give and receive support. This active participation strengthens the community and builds a collective knowledge base.

Online Engagement Checklist

- Identify Your Goals: What do you hope to gain from joining an online community? Whether it's support, information, or connection, knowing your goals can guide your interactions.
- Choose Your Platforms: Decide which platforms align best with your needs, whether it's Facebook groups, Reddit, or a mindfulness app.
- Set Boundaries: Define how much personal information you're comfortable sharing online, and stick to it.
- Contribute and Learn: Regularly engage with the community by sharing your experiences and learning from others.
- Stay Informed: Verify information with credible sources, and speak to a professional before taking any health advice.

THE POWER OF GROUP SESSIONS

When you sit in a room where everyone is there for the same purpose, the collective energy can jumpstart your personal healing. There's something comforting about being surrounded by others on similar paths, each bringing their energy and experiences to the shared space. This collective presence often leads to deeper emotional releases, as the group's energy can encourage you to let go of what no longer serves you. In these settings, you will hear stories and challenges that echo your own, and successes that inspire hope.

The structure of group somatic sessions is often carefully crafted to facilitate healing and connection. Typically, a skilled facilitator guides the session, creating a safe and supportive environment for participants. The facilitator will set the tone, ensuring everyone feels comfortable, and lead exercises encouraging connection and self-exploration.

Much like the exercises you do alone, common group activities might include breathing exercises. In these sessions, the synchronized breath of the group creates a rhythm that grounds and unites everyone. It's something you simply cannot experience while practicing alone.

Other times, movement exercises are used, inviting participants to express themselves physically and freeing emotions that might be trapped within. These activities encourage a sense of unity, as everyone moves or breathes in harmony, reinforcing the idea that healing is a communal process.

Participating in group sessions can require you to push beyond your comfort zone, challenging you to explore new facets of yourself. You might find yourself expressing emotions or trying techniques you wouldn't attempt alone. This willingness to be transparent with others opens the door for personal growth.

In the company of others, you will learn to give and receive support, creating personal bonds that strengthen your healing experience. The act of sharing can be incredibly liberating, reinforcing the idea that you're part of something larger than yourself.

WHERE TO BEGIN

So, how do you find and join a group session? Start by contacting local wellness centers or therapists specializing in somatic practices. If you are currently in talk therapy, your therapist may be able to suggest some resources to point you in the right direction.

Explore online directories dedicated to treatment and wellness. These directories often list local and virtual group therapy sessions, allowing you to find something that fits your needs and schedule. Don't hesitate to contact facilitators or organizers with questions about the sessions. Understanding the dynamics and expectations beforehand can help you feel more at ease when you join.

Group somatic sessions serve as a reminder that you're not alone. By stepping into this shared space, you acknowledge your desire for transformation and support from the energy and empathy of others.

As you continue on your somatic journey, remember that healing is an ongoing process directly related to the effort you put in and the connections you make along the way.

CHAPTER 15
REFLECTION AND INTEGRATION

"Life can only be understood backwards; but it must be lived forwards."

— SØREN KIERKEGAARD

The scene is easy to imagine. A person stands at the edge of a boundless lake, the mirror-like surface reflecting the cerulean sky above, and their face is reflected in the space between. This visual captures the essence of reflective journaling, a practice that asks you to see yourself, to understand the depths of your experiences, and to track the ripples of change as they spread through your life.

Reflective journaling is a tool for self-assessment and deeper self-awareness. By putting pen to paper, you create a space to explore your thoughts and feelings, unravel the complexities of your emotional world, and chart your somatic progress over time. It's an easy way to turn your inner thoughts into something you can see and comment on, helping you step back and better understand your experience.

Engaging in reflective journaling helps you gain clarity and understanding of your emotions and how they manifest in your body. This process of self-examination involves an intentional review of your actions and feelings, and their impacts on those around you.

The physical act of writing down your thoughts helps solidify your awareness, turning it into goal-directed action. By keeping a chronological record of your experiences, you create a timeline of your growth and evolution. This record becomes a testament to your resilience and the progress you've made. It allows you to revisit past moments, celebrate your achievements, and learn from the challenges you've overcome.

To guide your practice, consider using specific prompts encouraging you to examine and articulate your thoughts and feelings. Start by asking yourself:

- "What changes have you noticed in your body awareness since beginning somatic therapy?" Think about the subtle shifts in your physical sensations and how they've influenced your emotional state. Have you become more attuned to your body's signals or discovered new ways to respond to stress?
- "Describe a breakthrough or realization you experienced." Can you pinpoint or explore those moments that have transformed your understanding of yourself and your healing process?

- "What challenges have you overcome, and what strategies helped you?" This question encourages you to acknowledge your resilience and the tools you've developed to work through difficult situations.

Your journaling can be strictly organized by themes, topics, or emotions. Conversely, you can choose to keep your writing very organic and free, like a stream of consciousness. Whatever you choose, the biggest takeaway is to make it personal and achievable. Do not over-complicate the process to the point where you no longer use it as a tool.

If you are leaning toward themes that group entries by topics or emotions, this paragraph is for you. This approach allows you to identify patterns that emerge over time easily. Schedule periodic review sessions to read through your entries and process what you've documented. Look at recurring themes, celebrate your progress, and identify areas where you might want to focus more attention.

If you are considering a more freeform writing style, I've got you covered. There are many ways to track common themes and emotions as you progress. Personally, this is my preferred way of journaling, so I'll share my "organized but freeform" process with you.

1. **CHRONOLOGICAL** - I write in date order. My brain likes to see things chronologically, so my journaling is best kept that way. I find it helps me easily see how my emotions and practice progress day-to-day, and it is easier to spot hiccups that may cause me to go off course.
2. **ANNOTATED** - I have the ability to track emotions, events, topics, themes, and any other relevant things with colored tabs, sticky notes, paperclips, and other

annotating items you might have lying around. I use red tabs in areas where I am experiencing negative emotions and green tabs where I see growth. You might want to use a special color for things you want to research further, or emotions you can't identify. By creating a visual "key" in the front of my journal, I can see where those things pop up throughout my writing without sacrificing keeping things chronological.

3. **PERSONALIZED** - I make my journal a reflection of me. It could be a gorgeous cloth-bound book I purchase online, a plain spiral notebook from the school supply aisle, or a digital file I've carefully curated for my plan. I've used them all. The key is to make it your own. I love finding a doodle, a pressed flower, or a ticket stub between the pages. I've recently gotten into the habit of taping things in with washi tape or adding stickers. Sometimes, I write inspiring quotes with glitter markers, or pencil in the words from a meme. Everything matters when it comes to your healing journey. Mine happens to look very colorful, and that makes me happy.

Maintaining a consistent journaling practice is a valuable tool for ongoing growth and self-awareness. Aim to set a dedicated time each week to write, making it a regular part of your routine. This commitment will help you process emotions and experiences as they arise, preventing them from becoming overwhelming.

Reflective Journaling Workshop

To help you get started, try setting aside 10-20 minutes in a quiet space where you won't be interrupted. Use the prompts provided earlier as a guide, or whatever matches your needs today.

Write freely, without worrying about the way it looks. Don't think about your spelling, grammar, or sentence structure. Just let your thoughts flow naturally onto the page.

Once you've finished, take a deep breath. Read over what you've written. Highlight any observations or patterns that stand out and consider how they might inform your next steps.

This simple exercise may be something you do weekly or monthly as a way to track progress and growth.

INTEGRATING INSIGHTS INTO EVERYDAY LIFE

Let's pretend the lessons you've gathered from this book are like seeds. When planted in the garden of your daily life, they have the potential to grow into habits that nurture your mind and body. These lessons reveal their true power when they are applied. By putting what you've learned into everyday routines, you reinforce positive changes and lay the groundwork for continued healing.

It's about creating daily habits that implement the therapeutic wisdom you've gained, combined with small, consistent actions that align with your growth. This might mean starting your day with a grounding ritual that sets the tone for mindfulness or perhaps ending it with a calming practice that soothes the body and mind. As these habits become second nature, they serve as reminders of your progress, gently guiding you back to the path of growth whenever you stray.

These new revelations can also transform your relationships. With increased awareness of your emotions, you can communicate more effectively and empathetically with those around you. Perhaps you'll find yourself pausing before reacting in a heated moment, choosing to express your feelings calmly. Maybe you'll become more attuned to the emotions of those you care about, and you'll be able to support them in ways that have been emotionally inaccessible to you in the past. This type of "emotional intelligence" opens you to truly authentic connections.

Set intentions based on your growth goals, and let these guide your actions throughout the day. Perhaps you intend to practice patience, so you begin your morning with a few moments of stillness to center yourself. If you want to cultivate gratitude, you might end each day by thinking of three things you're thankful for.

I find this is a great way to unwind as I lie in bed each night. It puts me in a state of peace and thankfulness as I drift to sleep. Let these intentions anchor you, reminding you of the bigger picture even when life's chaos threatens to overwhelm.

To keep these findings at the forefront of your mind, use visual reminders, like sticky notes, to serve as gentle nudges throughout the day. You might use phrases like "Breathe deeply" or "Stay present" and display them where you'll see them often. Your desktop wallpaper and the lock screen on your cell are prime real estate locations for these messages. Digital reminders are handy as well. Consider setting phone alerts for mindfulness breaks, reminding you to pause, reflect, and recalibrate.

These small interruptions create space for mindfulness, breaking the cycle of reflexive behavior and inviting conscious choice. Over time, these reminders help solidify new habits, making it easier to integrate your somatic practices into your daily life.

One of my favorite ways to track progress is the Habit app. This free smartphone app works as a goal tracker and daily planner. It allows you to take all of the little things you want to do and find a way to incorporate them into your daily life. It's completely customizable, and includes self-motivation affirmations, reminders, tracking, weekly and monthly reports, and widgets.

I love the ability to share habits with friends or support group members. If you are working on common goals, you can nudge each other if you see someone falling behind. It's been a great way to bond with new friends and remain accountable while being supportive. It's perfect for ADHD brains, busy moms, and those losing focus due to brain fog from menopause. Whether you check one of those boxes or all of them, it's a great resource.

Personal, judgment-free, self-assessment plays a significant role in your development. Set aside time to consider what's working and what isn't, making adjustments as necessary. This ongoing evaluation gives you the clarity to adapt your practices to your evolving needs, ensuring they remain relevant and effective.

Life is dynamic, and so is your healing process. Embrace the ebb and flow of change, welcoming new perspectives and opportunities for growth as they present themselves.

CHAPTER 16
ADVANCED SOMATIC TECHNIQUES

"Do it again. Play it again. Sing it again. Read it again. Write it again. Sketch it again. Rehearse it again. Run it again. Try it again. Because again is practice, and practice is improvement, and improvement only leads to perfection."

— RICHELLE E. GOODRICH

Have you ever noticed how your body can hold onto the day's tensions, as if each muscle is a tight coil waiting to unwind? This sounds like a job for the advanced body scanning technique. We're peeling back all the layers of your hypothetical onion, and watching each layer reveal a new insight into your body's state of being.

Traditional body scans might already be familiar to you. Perhaps you've incorporated them into your regular practice as a way to relax at the end of a long day. But advanced body scanning asks you to go all in, turning up the dial on your somatic sensitivity and fully releasing your tension and negative emotion. Think of it as fine-tuning your body's awareness.

Differentiating between basic and advanced body scanning can be likened to the difference between a casual glance and a focused gaze. Basic scanning involves a broad sweep of attention over the body, acknowledging areas of tension and relaxation.

Advanced scanning, however, asks you to focus more intently, exploring each muscle, joint, and organ with curiosity and mindfulness. We want to notice the tense shoulder, but we really want to understand the layers of tension beneath it, tracing the sensation to its emotional root.

Often, emotions are stored in the body as micro-tensions, small knots of stress that we might not even be aware of. By honing in on these subtle sensations, advanced body scanning helps you uncover and release these deeply held emotions. It's like finding a little pocket of tension that's been expertly tucked away, and gently coaxing it to let go.

This process of focused awareness can lead to deep emotional processing and release. You might find tears welling up unexpectedly, or feel a sense of lightness as you release what you've been holding onto. This is your body's way of letting go and finding peace in the present moment. This level of awareness may be uncomfortable at first, but try to sit with those emotions, acknowledge them, and then release them.

To take this one step further, try incorporating breathwork into your body scanning practice. As you scan, guide your breath to the areas where you feel tension. See your breath as a gentle wave, soothing and relaxing those parts of your body. Synchronizing your breath with your body awareness will deepen your relaxation and strengthen your mind-body connection, bringing you a deep sense of calm.

> ## Practice Scan
>
> Let's do a practice scan together. Start by finding a comfortable position, either sitting or lying down. Close your eyes if you feel comfortable doing so. Take a few deep breaths to settle into the moment. As you begin your body scan, visualize a warm, glowing light starting at the top of your head, slowly working its way down your body. With each area, pause to notice any sensations. Are there layers of tension? What emotions might be tied to these feelings? As you move through your body, visualize each muscle, joint, and organ. Feel the tension and stress being carried away by the light. Spend a few moments with each area, willing your breath to guide the light deeper into any places of discomfort. Notice any emotions that arise and let them flow freely without judgment. Picture your body softening as you release the tension.

By practicing advanced body scanning regularly, you can uncover hidden tensions and experience deeper emotional healing. This type of engagement with your body is a way to experience physical and emotional release in a nurturing and compassionate way.

SOMATIC EXPERIENCING: DEEP DIVE INTO HEALING

Somatic experiencing is a unique path that focuses on the body being a powerful tool for processing trauma. Developed by Peter

A. Levine, this approach recognizes that trauma isn't just an emotional or psychological issue; it's deeply embedded in our physiology.

You already know that you carry the weight of past experiences in your thoughts, but the same is true in your muscles and nerves. Somatic experiencing helps you track these bodily sensations and release the pent-up energy that trauma often traps inside.

Unlike traditional talk therapies that might dive directly into the emotional aspects, somatic experiencing begins with the body's story, using physical sensations as a guide. This method acknowledges that sometimes words aren't enough, and our bodies have their own wisdom and language, waiting to be uncovered.

There are several foundational principles that work to guide the healing process. One principle is pendulation, which involves moving between states of comfort and discomfort. Think of it as a gentle shift between safety and challenge when exploring painful memories. This shifting back and forth gives your nervous system time to find balance. It's like dipping your toes into a cold pool before fully immersing yourself. It's a safe way to gradually acclimate and build resilience.

Then there's titration, which breaks down traumatic experiences into manageable pieces. This technique keeps your system from becoming overwhelmed so that you can process trauma in small, digestible parts. By taking things slowly, you can avoid becoming retraumatized, which is a fear that keeps many from seeking therapy to begin with.

Resourcing is another aspect that focuses on developing internal and external support systems to provide safety and stability.

Think of these resources as your anchors, grounding you when the emotional seas get rough.

Somatic experiencing can produce radical shifts in trauma symptoms and overall wellness. You may begin to notice a reduction in PTSD symptoms, such as intrusive thoughts and hypervigilance, giving you a greater sense of control over your body and emotions. You'll start reclaiming the parts of yourself that trauma has overshadowed so you can feel whole and connected.

This internal shift translates into everyday life, as you gain confidence in your ability to cope with stress and adversity. You may discover a sense of freedom as you consider a future no longer defined by past traumas, but built upon the strength you've found within yourself. Girl power!

INTEGRATING SOMATIC PRACTICES WITH OTHER THERAPIES

Somatic healing is not a cookie-cutter process. In fact, it's strongly encouraged that you craft the perfect plan for *your* lifestyle, *your* hobbies, and *your* strengths. Sometimes, that means that you need more than one approach to address all the layers of your life. Let's touch on a few options below.

Let's consider the effectiveness of combining somatic therapy and cognitive-behavioral therapy (CBT). While CBT helps you identify and change negative thought patterns, somatic practices bring attention to the physical sensations accompanying these thoughts. Together, they provide an in-depth way to address both mind and body.

Consider the impact of working through a challenging thought pattern in talk therapy, then using a somatic technique to release the physical tension associated with that thought. That's the power of combining therapies.

Integrating body-focused practices with traditional talk therapy is another way to grow your therapeutic experience. For example, trauma-focused therapies like Eye Movement Desensitization and Reprocessing (EMDR) can be enhanced with somatic practices. You might discuss a painful memory in a session with your therapist, and then use somatic exercises to process the physical sensations and release trapped emotions. This tag-team approach can be essential for reducing PTSD symptoms.

Incorporating mindfulness-based stress reduction (MBSR) with somatic exercises is another powerful combination. MBSR focuses on present-moment awareness, complementing somatic practices that engage the body. Consider using MBSR to manage anxiety. Adding somatic exercise helps to ground the body, enhancing the calming effects of mindfulness. The combination offers a more therapeutic approach in addressing the mind's chatter and the body's tension.

Skilled practitioners can guide you in creating a treatment plan that aligns with your goals and needs. But, it doesn't stop there. You may notice your approach expanding to a collaboration where therapists, bodyworkers, and other specialists work together to support your healing. It's like having a team of experts all focused on your specific needs, each bringing their unique skills to the table. Go team!

What's a bodyworker?

Bodyworkers are trained professionals who use hands-on techniques to help the body heal and feel better. They work with muscles, joints, and energy pathways through methods like massage, acupressure, and reflexology. By applying pressure, stretching, or gentle touch, they help relieve pain, reduce stress, and improve circulation. Bodywork supports the body's natural healing process, helping people feel more balanced, relaxed, and connected to themselves physically.

Creating a personalized integrative approach requires time and experimentation. List your therapy goals and consider how somatic practices can support them.

Perhaps you want to reduce anxiety or improve emotional regulation. Try aligning these goals with specific somatic techniques that complement each other and work toward that end result. For example, you might try pairing a breathing exercise with a cognitive restructuring technique or using movement practices alongside meditation. Or, if you're like me, you might find success by incorporating guided imagery into your EMDR therapy. Don't be afraid to experiment with different combinations to find what works best. It's all about finding the right mix for you.

Integrating somatic practices with other therapies is important to customize your path forward. Somatic healing is a highly flexible process that offers something for everyone and can adapt to your evolving needs. As you explore these combinations, you'll likely discover new ways to connect with yourself and others.

CHAPTER 17
MAINTAINING MOMENTUM

"Momentum begets momentum, and the best way to start is to start."

— GIL PENCHINA

When you're standing at the foot of a towering mountain looking up at the path ahead, the climb seems daunting and unreachable, but look how far you've come already! Each step you've taken represents a learned experience, a moment of growth, or a challenge you've overcome. This is what maintaining momentum in your somatic practice feels like. It's about keeping the rhythm, even when the climb feels steep.

You've already laid a solid foundation; now it's time to ensure that this practice continues to serve you in the long run, providing stability and growth in your everyday life.

SUSTAINING YOUR SOMATIC PRACTICE FOR LONG-TERM WELLNESS

Consistency, Consistency, consistency. Regular practice is not recommended; it's necessary for ongoing progress. Think about brushing your teeth or taking a shower. These are daily routines that contribute to your overall health. Similarly, incorporating somatic exercises into your daily or weekly routine can directly impact your emotional and physical health. By establishing a routine that works with your schedule, you create a structure that supports your healing...even on the days when motivation is low.

Start small by setting aside specific times for your somatic exercises, whether it's a few minutes in the morning or a dedicated session each week. Building habits around these practices ensures they become a natural part of your daily life, much like drinking your morning coffee or winding down with a book at night.

Maintaining motivation can be challenging, especially when life throws curveballs your way. Sometimes, you'll feel like you're making progress; other times, you might feel stuck. To keep your motivation high, it's important to set achievable goals and celebrate small victories along the way.

You don't have to climb the entire mountain in one go. Instead, focus on reaching the next milestone, whether that's mastering a new technique or noticing a subtle change in how you feel. Celebrating these wins helps to reinforce your commitment to the practice and provides a sense of accomplishment.

Additionally, consider using motivational tools like vision boards or progress charts. Vision boards tap into your creative side to provide powerful reminders of your dreams, affirmations, and goals. Your vision board keeps your aspirations at the forefront of your mind. Don't have a vision board? No problem. It's a great art therapy project for your somatic journey. Consider what you might include on yours and set aside a time to make that your first creative therapy session.

Progress charts, on the other hand, give you a tangible way to track your growth with a visual representation of how far you've come. These charts can start off simple in the beginning, focusing on the areas where motivation is needed, and become more goal-oriented as you move forward in your practice. They are perfect for the ADHD girlies who love to tick off the boxes of a list.

As with any meaningful pursuit, obstacles will shake your confidence and leave you questioning whether you should give up. By the way, the answer to that is, "No!" Time management is a common hurdle, as busy schedules can make it challenging to prioritize self-care. Structured scheduling can be a lifesaver for addressing this.

Treat your somatic exercises as appointments that you can't miss. Block out time in your calendar and treat it with the same importance as a doctor's appointment or work meeting. If you do happen to miss a scheduled exercise, don't worry about it. It's not an all-or-nothing process. Progress is progress. Just take a deep breath and move on to the next step.

Another effective strategy is to find an accountability partner who will help you stay dedicated to your goal. Whether it's a friend, family member, or a group of like-minded individuals, having someone to share your thoughts with can make all the difference. They can provide support during tough times, celebrate your successes, and act as a sounding board in times of need.

Keeping your somatic practice fresh and exciting is a **HUGE** factor in sustaining momentum. It's easy to fall into a routine and feel like you're going through the motions without any real engagement. To prevent stagnation, explore new somatic exercises or techniques that challenge you in different ways.

Seasonal and environmental changes can also provide inspiration. A walk in the crisp autumn air or a sunrise meditation can invigorate your practice. By embracing change and variety, you keep your practice dynamic and engaging, promoting a sense of curiosity and continuous learning.

Somatic Practice Exploration

Consider this checklist as a guide to help you maintain and expand your somatic practice. Use it to explore new exercises, set goals, and review your progress:

- Identify a new somatic exercise or technique you'd like to try.
- Schedule dedicated time for your practice and mark it in your calendar.
- Set a small, achievable goal for your somatic practice this week.
- Create a vision board or progress chart to visualize your goals and your accomplishments.
- Find an accountability partner or support group to share your experiences.
- Experiment with practicing in different environments or during different times of the day.
- Evaluate your practice at the end of each week, noting any positive changes or areas of concern.

Your somatic practice is an evolving tool, so let it grow with you. The positive changes will energize you to keep moving forward.

Your pain is valid. Your trauma is real. You are worthy of the freedom and peace that comes from deep somatic healing. Remember, this is your path; every step forward is a testament to your strength and resilience. I believe in you. Now it's your turn to believe in yourself, too.

AFTERWORD

"The final stage of healing is using what happened to you to help other people."

— GLORIA STEINEM

My vision for this book has always been to inspire and equip you to reclaim your body and heal your heart. I hope you found clear, easy-to-read information that resonates with your life experiences, making healing feel more accessible and relatable, without getting lost in complex medical terminology.

As we reach the end of our time together, let's take a moment to review what we've learned about trauma and healing. By bringing awareness to the mind-body connection, embracing creative expression, and crafting personalized routines, you can transform your relationship with your body and heal your heart from the past.

AFTERWORD

Throughout this book, we've explored how your body holds the key to understanding and releasing trauma. From the gentle techniques of somatic awareness to the expressive freedom of art and movement, you now have a toolkit to help guide you. Remember, the exercises and techniques we've discussed are theoretical and practical steps to motivate yourself daily.

One of your greatest assets is the power of community and support. Healing doesn't happen in isolation. Surround yourself with people who support and understand you. Whether it's a local group, an online forum, or a supportive friend, these connections will boost your resilience and encourage you when you need it most.

I want you to take action. Set small, achievable goals for integrating these practices into your life. Reflect regularly on your progress and celebrate even the smallest victories. Find joy. Seek it out.

Friends, this book is a resource. It's a starting point. It's not the only way forward. We've only briefly touched on some of the amazing things somatic practices can achieve. Keep exploring these practices. Stay open to new resources. Attend workshops. Join support groups. Buy the coloring book. Find a fantastic therapist. Sign up for the dance class. Dive into the science. This is your life. Never stop looking for ways to craft it into the life you want.

Healing is a journey, not a destination.

I am so proud of you for taking the first step. Thank you for trusting me to be part of your process. Your participation with this material shows your commitment to healing. It takes such

AFTERWORD

incredible courage to begin, and it is my sincere wish for your continued growth and healing.

Please share your experiences with others on similar paths. Share your success with women everywhere. You never know what someone can gain from your personal story. Your voice matters, and your transparency can inspire others. Be brave.

Wishing you the brightest days ahead.

Make a Difference with Your Review

Help Other Women Heal, One Word at a Time

"The best way to find yourself is to lose yourself in the service of others."

— MAHATMA GANDHI

When we take a moment to help others, without expecting anything in return, it lifts us all up.

If *Somatic Healing for Women* helped you feel more grounded, seen, or supported, would you take a moment to help someone else who's just starting out on their journey?

So many women are curious about healing...but don't know where to begin. My goal is to make somatic healing simple, gentle, and welcoming for every woman...no matter her background or story.

But here's the truth: most people pick a book based on the reviews. That means *your* words could be the reason someone

MAKE A DIFFERENCE WITH YOUR REVIEW

takes their first step toward healing. You have the power to help change someone's life. That's pretty impressive.

Your review might help:

- one woman trust her body again.

- one mom finally take a breath.

- one survivor feel less alone.

- one person say yes to healing.

- one heart feel hope again.

If you love lifting others up…hey, bestie. You're my kind of person. Please take a moment to leave a review wherever you buy books. If the book was gifted to you, or if you checked it out from your local library, you can leave a review on Goodreads, Amazon, The StoryGraph, Fable, Instagram…wherever you share all the things.

Thank you, from the bottom of my healing heart.

– R.V. Brown

Author of *Somatic Healing for Women*

COMING SOON

Somatic Healing for Women Workbook + Journal

Join the mailing list at: SomaticHealingForWomen.com

Follow along on Instagram: @SomaticHealingForWomen

REFERENCES

- 3X Health. (n.d.). *The science behind consistency: How it rewires your brain for success.* https://3xhealth.com/the-science-behind-consistency-how-it-rewires-your-brain-for-success/
- Ackerman, C. E. (2022, March 8). Cognitive restructuring techniques for reframing thoughts. *PositivePsychology.com.* https://positivepsychology.com/cbt-cognitive-restructuring-cognitive-distortions/
- Ackerman, C. E. (2022, December 8). Mindfulness at work: Create calm & focus in the workplace. *PositivePsychology.com.* https://positivepsychology.com/mindfulness-at-work/
- Ackerman, C. E. (2023, April 11). The neuroscience of gratitude and effects on the brain. *PositivePsychology.com.* https://positivepsychology.com/neuroscience-of-gratitude/
- Alegría, M., Atkins, M., Farmer, E., Slaton, E., & Stelk, W. (2010). One size does not fit all: Taking diversity, culture and context seriously. *Administration and Policy in Mental Health and Mental Health Services Research, 37,* 48–60. https://pmc.ncbi.nlm.nih.gov/articles/PMC2874609/
- American Psychiatric Association. (n.d.). Healing through art. https://www.psychiatry.org/news-room/apa-blogs/healing-through-art
- Anxious Minds. (n.d.). Mindfulness body scan. https://www.anxiousminds.co.uk/guide-to-mindfulness-body-scan/
- Art Therapy Resources. (n.d.). The power of metaphors and symbols in art therapy. https://arttherapyresources.com.au/metaphors-and-symbols/
- Bay Area CBT Center. (n.d.). Somatic experiencing in CBT: Enhancing trauma treatment. https://bayareacbtcenter.com/the-role-of-somatic-experiencing-in-cbt/#:~:text=Integrating%20CBT%20and%20somatic%20therapy,experiencing%20and%20trauma%20restorative%20care
- BetterMe. (n.d.). Somatic bedtime routine: How it helps and what it looks like. https://betterme.world/articles/somatic-bedtime-routine/

REFERENCES

- Boyd, J. E., Lanius, R. A., & McKinnon, M. C. (2018). Mindfulness-based treatments for posttraumatic stress disorder: A review of the treatment literature and neurobiological evidence. *Psychiatric Research,* 262, 440–451. https://pmc.ncbi.nlm.nih.gov/articles/PMC5747539/
- Brody, J. E. (2017, October 30). Trying the Feldenkrais Method for chronic pain. *The New York Times.* https://www.nytimes.com/2017/10/30/well/trying-the-feldenkrais-method-for-chronic-pain.html
- By Repose. (n.d.). Somatic experiences of marginalized identities: Navigating intersectionality through healing. https://byrepose.com/journal/somatic-experiences-of-marginalized-identities-navigating-intersectionality-through-healing
- Cherney, K. (2019, August 21). Progressive muscle relaxation: Benefits, how-to, technique. *Healthline.* https://www.healthline.com/health/progressive-muscle-relaxation
- Cleveland Clinic. (n.d.). Biofeedback: What it is, purpose, procedure, risks & benefits. https://my.clevelandclinic.org/health/treatments/13354-biofeedback
- Counselling in Alberta. (n.d.). The power of emotional self-regulation: Nurturing your mental well-being. https://counsellinginalberta.com/blog/the-power-of-emotional-self-regulation-nurturing-your-mental-well-being
- Drarielleschwartz.com. (n.d.). *Embodiment in trauma recovery.* https://drarielleschwartz.com/embodiment-in-trauma-recovery/
- Emotions Market. (n.d.). 20 types of somatic therapy and their benefits. https://emotions.market/blog/20-types-of-somatic-therapy-and-their-benefits/
- Harvard Health Publishing. (2022, October 13). Mindfulness meditation to control pain. https://www.health.harvard.edu/pain/mindfulness-meditation-to-control-pain
- Inspire Malibu. (n.d.). Exploring the evidence behind somatic therapy. https://www.inspiremalibu.com/blog/mental-health/evidence-behind-somatic-therapy-is-it-truly-effective/
- Johns Hopkins Medicine. (n.d.). Somatic self care | Office of Well-Being. https://www.hopkinsmedicine.org/office-of-well-being/connection-support/somatic-self-care
- Kirstein, M. (n.d.). 12 effective somatic therapy exercises for holistic healing. https://www.monakirstein.com/somatic-therapy-exercises/

REFERENCES

- Life Catalyst. (n.d.). The therapeutic power of vision boards in goal achievement. https://lifecatalystct.com/the-therapeutic-power-of-vision-boards-in-goal-achievement/
- Mayo Clinic Press. (n.d.). Mind-body connection: Ancient wisdom meets modern science. https://mcpress.mayoclinic.org/living-well/mind-body-connection-ancient-wisdom-meets-modern-science/
- Medina, J. (2022, November 22). Somatic therapy can heal the imprints of trauma. *Los Angeles Times*. https://www.latimes.com/california/newsletter/2022-11-22/group-therapy-body-somatics-trauma-group-therapy
- Medical News Today. (2021, October 29). Mindfulness and emotional well-being: Strategies to try. https://www.medicalnewstoday.com/articles/mindfulness-for-mental-wellbeing
- Medical News Today. (2023, January 12). Pain management: Physical methods and techniques. https://www.medicalnewstoday.com/articles/pain-management-techniques#physical-methods
- Merriam-Webster. (n.d.). Pseudoscience. In *Merriam-Webster.com dictionary*. https://www.merriam-webster.com/dictionary/pseudoscience
- Mindful. (n.d.). How to manage stress with mindfulness and meditation. https://www.mindful.org/how-to-manage-stress-with-mindfulness-and-meditation/
- Mindful Health Solutions. (n.d.). Emotional triggers: Why they matter & how to manage them effectively. https://mindfulhealthsolutions.com/emotional-triggers-why-they-matter-how-to-manage-them-effectively/
- Mindfulness Exercises. (n.d.). An advanced body scan meditation script. https://mindfulnessexercises.com/body-scan-advanced/
- Mindfulness Skills for Trauma and PTSD: Body Scan .... (psychotherapyacademy.org). (n.d.). https://psychotherapyacademy.org/courses/dialectical-behavior-therapy-for-trauma-the-case-of-maria/modules/treatment-formulation-mindfulness-and-distress-tolerance-skills/section/mindfulness-skills-for-trauma-and-ptsd-body-scan-mindfulness-of-the-five-senses-breathing-and-enjoyable-activities/
- Monakirstein.com. (n.d.). Somatic therapy exercises. https://www.monakirstein.com/somatic-therapy-exercises/

REFERENCES

- Native Clinics. (n.d.). How somatic therapy can help you manage chronic pain. https://nativeclinics.com/how-somatic-therapy-can-help-you-manage-chronic-pain/
- Ogunyemi, L. (n.d.). Understanding the hidden struggles: Cultural and somatic expressions of depression and anxiety in Black women. *Auctores Online*. https://www.auctoresonline.org/article/understanding-the-hidden-struggles-cultural-and-somatic-expressions-of-depression-and-anxiety-in-black-women
- Payne, P., Levine, P. A., & Crane-Godreau, M. A. (2015). Somatic experiencing: Effectiveness and key factors of a body-oriented therapy approach. *Frontiers in Psychology, 6*, 93. https://pmc.ncbi.nlm.nih.gov/articles/PMC8276649/
- Payne, P., Levine, P. A., & Crane-Godreau, M. A. (2015). Somatic experiencing for posttraumatic stress disorder: A review of evidence and case studies. *Frontiers in Psychology, 6*, 93. https://pmc.ncbi.nlm.nih.gov/articles/PMC5518443/
- PositivePsychology.com. (n.d.). Journaling prompts. https://positivepsychology.com/journaling-prompts/
- PositivePsychology.com. (n.d.). Motivational interviewing: 30+ tools, affirmations & more. https://positivepsychology.com/motivational-interviewing-exercises/
- Psych Central. (n.d.). 4 at-home somatic therapy exercises for trauma recovery. https://psychcentral.com/lib/somatic-therapy-exercises-for-trauma
- Psychotherapy.net. (n.d.). Peter Levine on trauma healing: A somatic approach. https://www.psychotherapy.net/interview/interview-peter-levine
- Ptsduk.org. (n.d.). Music therapy for PTSD. https://www.ptsduk.org/music-therapy-for-ptsd/
- Sandstonecare.com. (n.d.). Somatic therapy | Understanding the mind-body connection. https://www.sandstonecare.com/blog/somatic-therapy/
- Seacrest Recovery Center. (n.d.). How can I integrate the insights and lessons from therapy into my daily life and recovery practices? https://seacrestrecoverycenteroh.com/how-can-i-integrate-the-insights-and-lessons-from-therapy-into-my-daily-life-and-recovery-practices/

REFERENCES

- Segerstrom, S. C., & Miller, G. E. (2004). Current directions in stress and human immune function. *Psychological Bulletin, 130*(4), 601–630. https://pmc.ncbi.nlm.nih.gov/articles/PMC4465119/
- Sheppard Pratt. (n.d.). Dance/movement therapy | Knowledge Center. https://www.sheppardpratt.org/knowledge-center/treatment/dance-movement-therapy/#:~:text=She%20reached%20them%20through%20the,steps%20(Chaiklin%2C%201979)
- Somatic Experiencing® International. (n.d.). Somatic Experiencing: Supporting trauma resolution and resilience. https://traumahealing.org/
- Somatic Movement Center. (n.d.). Somatic Movement Center® student testimonials. https://somaticmovementcenter.com/somatics-testimonials/
- Somatic Therapy vs. Talk Therapy: Which is Right for You?. (n.d.). Nativeclinics.com. https://nativeclinics.com/somatic-therapy-vs-talk-therapy-which-is-right-for-you/
- Stress symptoms: Effects on your body and behavior. (n.d.). Mayo Clinic. https://www.mayoclinic.org/healthy-lifestyle/stress-management/in-depth/stress-symptoms/art-20050987
- Taylor, S. E. (2011). The role of social support in coping with psychological stress. *Current Directions in Psychological Science, 20*(1), 53–58. https://pmc.ncbi.nlm.nih.gov/articles/PMC9534006/
- The Best 5-Senses Grounding Techniques for Anxiety Relief. (n.d.). PsychCentral. https://psychcentral.com/anxiety/using-the-five-senses-for-anxiety-relief
- The Human Condition. (n.d.). Writing therapy: Types, benefits, and effectiveness. https://thehumancondition.com/writing-therapy/
- This Feeling Human. (n.d.). How our bodies remember what our minds try to forget. https://www.thisfeelinghuman.com/post/echoes-of-experience-how-our-bodies-remember-what-our-minds-try-to-forget
- University of Miami Health System. (n.d.). Fatigue. https://umiamihealth.org/treatments-and-services/uhealth-comprehensive-women%E2%80%99s-health-alliance/women%27s-services/primary-care/ten-common-health-complaints-for-us-women?utm_source=chatgpt.com
- Uclahealth.org. (n.d.). Free moving dance has healing benefits for people with mental health concerns. https://www.uclahealth.org/news/

REFERENCES

article/free-moving-dance-has-healing-benefits-for-people-with-mental-health-concerns
- Van der Kolk, B. A., & Lanius, R. A. (2023). The body keeps the score: The neurobiological profile of trauma and posttraumatic stress. *Neuroscience & Biobehavioral Reviews, 143*, 104944. https://www.sciencedirect.com/science/article/pii/S0149763423000027
- Verywellmind.com. (n.d.). 5-4-3-2-1 grounding technique. https://www.verywellmind.com/5-4-3-2-1-grounding-technique-8639390
- Wellman Psychology. (2019, August 22). Benefits of reflective journaling. https://wellmanpsychology.com/mindbodyblog/2019/8/22/benefits-of-reflective-journaling

www.ingramcontent.com/pod-product-compliance
Lightning Source LLC
Chambersburg PA
CBHW050522100526
44581CB00002B/80